CATALAN PAINTING

CATALAN PAINTING

From the Nineteenth to the Surprising Twentieth Century

JOAN AINAUD DE LASARTE

SKIRA

RIZZOLI
NEW YORK

Under the honorary auspices
of the Department of Culture
GENERALITAT OF CATALONIA

Work published under the auspices of
the United Nations Educational Scientific,
and Cultural Organization.

© 1992 by Editions d'Art Albert Skira S.A., Geneva

Published in the United States of America in 1992 by

Rizzoli INTERNATIONAL PUBLICATIONS, INC.
300 Park Avenue South/New York 10010

Translated from the Spanish by Michael Heron

ISBN 0-8478-1558-7
LC 89-43605

Printed in Switzerland

CONTENTS

Pablo Ruiz Picasso (1881-1973). Life, Barcelona, 1903 (197 × 127).
The Cleveland Museum of Art.

INTRODUCTION

Even though each of the three volumes devoted to Catalan painting and Catalonia adopts a distinct approach, the three offer an obvious relationship as a trilogy.

The first volume dealing with Romanesque art took as its starting point the actual works, grouped for easier understanding although in a way that inevitably proved conventional. In the second, the artists' names were often fleshed out by biographical material, yet insight into their ideas and aims was not possible. In this third volume, however, alongside the works treated we shall hear the artists' own voice, as well as that of critics, commentators and contemporary poets and prose writers.

So in the present case, the elements one might draw on to form an opinion are far more complete and abundant, although their very abundance forces us to limit an originally much higher figure. Let us bear in mind that the census of painters registered in Catalonia between the nineteenth and twentieth centuries exceeds 7,000. Moreover, we are faced with another convention, that of representing artists' often varied production, over more than fifty years in not a few instances, by a single work that manifests but one moment or manner marking their plastic expression.

As with literary anthologies, there is a great difference between making a selection based on *established* artists with a life's work behind them and one including certain young painters who may be at an early or incomplete stage in their œuvre. At all events, I prefer risking the ever-adventurous mission of a *prophet* in an attempt to bring my selection up to the present, rather than adopting the less compromising position of those who contemplate artistic forms and manners from the past.

Of course the inclusion of certain artists within the sphere of Catalan culture remains arguable, although it seems obvious to us that they had to be mentioned, especially when given their individual importance or relationship to other artists. Picasso's case is, I think, the most outstanding, but there are others, for example that of Joaquim Torres Garcia (Catalan on his father's side). On the other hand, I shall refer more briefly to other painters who worked sporadically in Catalonia, although they maintained friendships and personal relations here. We might recall in this respect Vicenç Rodes, a native of Alicante and author of excellent pastel portraits, and the Provençal Josep Flaugier—both artists connected with the School of Llotja —or the Mexicans Francisco Goitia and Diego Rivera. Several of the most important French painters of the early twentieth century, Henri Matisse, André Derain and Raoul Dufy for example, spent some time in the Roussillon, the Empordà and the Vallès whereas at various periods during the First Word War and the 30s Tossa and Barcelona were home to artists such as Olga Sacharoff, Tristan Tzara, Marie Laurencin, Francis Picabia, Marc Chagall, André Masson, Georges Kars, Oscar Zügel and Jean Metzinger.

On the other hand, we should not forget the activity of native Catalans on the Balearic Isles and in many centres outside the region, principally Madrid, Paris and Rome, as well as in other areas of Spain, Italy, Germany and England, not to mention the presence of Catalan artists beyond Europe, in Mexico, the United States, Brazil, Argentina, Algeria and other countries of America, Africa and Asia.

The requirements of this edition force me to reduce considerably commentary on artists who were basically illustrators—a very important branch of Catalan art—or the partial devotion to the painting of others who, in the main, distinguished themselves in other fields of the plastic arts.

HISTORICAL BACKGROUND

To describe the artistic life of Catalonia throughout the nineteenth and twentieth centuries I have to recall, albeit in broad outline, a series of determining factors that were the product of not only political events but also socio-political conditions.

Let us begin with the former. The consequences of the French Revolution would lead, beginning in 1793, to what would come to be known as the *Guerra Gran* (literally the Great War) in Catalonia. This war represents not only a political and military break between the Spanish monarchy and the French Republic, but also ecclesiastical division, when the Val d'Aran passed from the (suppressed) diocese of Comenge to that of Urgell as compensation for the part of Cerdagne that remained within territories under French administration.

The Napoleonic Wars were known in Catalonia as the French War. Hostilities were relatively brief, lasting from the occupation of the country in 1808 by General Duhesme until the negociated evacuation of 1814, but it was a hard-fought conflict and had serious consequences. The belligerents, both French and Spanish, shifted from superficial flattery of the Catalans to suspicion and distrust. One of the most important figures in contemporary artistic circles was the Provençal painter Josep Flaugier who, appointed Director of the School of Llotja, would in fact save many works of art from monasteries suppressed by the French authorities following the example of the Revolution, whereas Montserrat Monastery, to name but one example, was actually burnt down in 1810 during wartime manœuvres.

The period beginning with the restoration of the reign of Ferdinand VII until his death (1814-1833) represents a succession of conflicts: the liberal triennium (1821-1823), the absolutist reaction (1822) and the invasion in 1823 by the duke of Angoulême's troops dispatched by the Congress of Vienna to support the absolutists who had installed the so-called Regency of Urgell in Catalonia. The monasteries were suppressed once again in 1821.

As a result of the French Revolution's tactic of suppressing historical territorial divisions and replacing them by *départements* based on more or less arbitrary geographical divisions, the counties ceded to France in the seventeenth century became, in 1790, the Département of the Pyrénées-Orientales, taking their place within an overall division now known as Languedoc-Roussillon. Following Napoleon's invasion of the Iberian peninsula, the rest of Catalonia was also divided into *départements* which, as of 1810, had Barcelona, Reus and the Seu d'Urgell as their capitals. After various alternatives were tried, they were called «provinces» in 1822, with Barcelona, Girona, Tarragona and Lleida as capitals. Suppressed in 1823, they were reestablished in 1833 and have existed in this form until the present day, although in 1913 the Spanish State accepted a federation or *Mancomunitat* of the four Catalan provinces, abolished in 1924. The Second Republic (1931-1939) brought with it the *de facto* temporary abolition of the provinces, which were subsequently reestablished with the suppression of Catalonia's autonomy in 1939. In 1977 an autonomous structure was superimposed in a rather contradictory fashion on this political and administrative framework.

We should also recall that concurrently with the Napoleonic invasion, independence movements in Spain's South American colonies, beginning to gather momentum as of 1810, would eventually triumph in 1824, excepting Cuba and Puerto Rico which would only separate definitively from the mother country in 1898. Of major importance for Catalonia were imports of American cotton and trade in other products, as well as the return of Catalan emigrants from America. One of their most representative figures was Josep Xifré (Arenys de Mar, 1777 - Barcelona, 1856), who divided his activities between Cuba and New York. The Maresme and the Penedès were among the regions that benefited most from this commercial and industrial situation.

Upon the death of Ferdinand VII, a situation of permanent conflict broke out together with the first Carlist war, which owes its name to the person of Ferdinand's brother, Carlos María Isidro, proclaimed king of Spain instead of his niece Isabella II, who was entrusted during her minority to the regency of her mother, María Cristina. This phase lasted seven years (1833-1840) in the course of which, in 1835, the nation's convents were suppressed and burnt down, their patrimony subsequently destroyed or sold for the benefit of speculators. I should point out that a historian as little in favour of Carlism as Karl Marx recognized the popular rural basis of traditional Carlism as opposed to the so-called *liberalismo* fomented by the militarists, capitalist tradespeople and speculators, the aristocracy with vast estates (almost non-existent in Catalonia) and the interests of those who had speculated with the secularized property of the Church.

The end of the second Carlist war (1846-1849), also known as the *Guerra dels Matiners* (War of the Early Risers), saw the advent of a period centred, in the international sphere, on the empire of Napoleon III (1852-1870), who married the Spaniard Eugenia de Montijo in 1853.

One of the major figures in Spanish politics of this time was General Joan Prim, born at Reus in 1814. In 1860 he distinguished himself in the Moroccan War, an episode that emulated the French campaigns in Algeria, and in 1862 assumed command of an international expedition bound for Mexico, an adventure from which he would disentangle himself in the face of French ambitions. He also played an outstanding role in the September Revolution of 1868 which caused the overthrow of Isabella II and the designation of Amadeo of Savoy as king of Spain.

The assassination of General Prim (1870), the abdication of Amadeo and the proclamation of the Republic, two presidents of which were Catalan, Estanislau Figueras and Francesc Pi i Margall, set in motion a long period of political instability. It was at this time, amid the third and last Carlist war (1872-1876) that Baldomer Lostau proclaimed the *Estat Català* (Catalan State) in 1873. The exhaustion and discouragement of the belligerents led in the end to the restoration of the Bourbon monarchy in the person of Alfonso XII (1876), with the support of middle-class Catalans such as Manuel Girona.

Between 1853 and 1856 the Crimean War broke out in eastern Europe and was followed with considerable interest by the Catalans. This should come as no surprise, because for centuries the main centre supplying wheat to Catalonia, chronically short of that cereal, was the *black lands* of the Ukraine. The prolonged suppression of this route was to play a fundamental role in strengthening the internal Spanish market, inasmuch as wheat from Castile was exchanged for Catalan textile products.

The city walls of Barcelona and its fortress, raised to watch over the city and not to defend it, were demolished in 1855. These events, together with the plans for the internal development of Barcelona and other cities, which put to use the building space created as convents were torn down, made possible extraordinary urban growth, encouraged even further by the fact that many families living in the country preferred the comfort and safety of the cities in a time of war and upheaval.

A very significant feature of the Restoration period was the Barcelona Universal Exhibition of 1888, which put the Catalan capital on the itinerary of the great industrial fairs begun in London in 1851 and stimulated by competition with Paris, New York, Munich, Vienna, Philadelphia, Sydney, Amsterdam and New Orleans.

Along with this industrial expansion, important workers' movements were organized, some with communist and socialist tendencies, others of a nihilist and anarchist nature, but all of international scope and firmly implanted in the Catalan industrial centres, not only in the large cities of the region, but also in the industrial ventures nestled in the valleys of certain rivers, where new sources of energy were sought, especially hydroelectric power, which was complementing steam.

Politicians often felt cut off from the guidelines of the parties with a national basis. In Manresa in 1892, an assembly put forward the foundations for so-called *political Catalanism*, drawing upon precedents of a variety of tendencies that had already come to light on the occasion of the 1868 revolution.

The independence movements in Cuba and the Philippines, with the assistance of the United States, had an immediate effect on the Catalans settled in those islands. It was for this reason that General Prim, shortly before his assassination, had tried to reach an agreement with the Cubans, while other political forces, for example the federalists of Pi i Margall undertook similar negociations. Nevertheless, the repressive attitude of the military leaders prevented any peaceful solution. War broke out and Cuba's independence was recognized by the Treaty of Paris (1898). The United States set up a base there at Guantánamo which still exists, placing Puerto Rico under a special, temporary regime although the island now enjoys the status of a free associated state. As for the Philippines, they remained a colony of the United States until 1946.

In 1901 the central Spanish government sent—adequately funded for his mission—a professional agitator, Alejandro Lerroux, to Catalonia with the express purpose of fomentting discontent in Catalan political circles. In 1906 a coalition of parties called *Solidaritat Catalana* (Catalan Solidarity) won a great electoral victory. In the following year Enric Prat de la Riba was nominated President of the *Diputación* of Barcelona and if in 1909 the events of the *Semana Trágica* or Tragic Week (deaths, fires, repression by means of executions) brought him great difficulties, nonetheless in 1913 he successfully established an administrative body common to the four Catalan provinces, the *Mancomunitat*, which would survive his death in 1917. It proved difficult, however, to replace him, mainly owing to terrorism by both workers and industrialists. In 1923 the *coup d'état* by General Miguel Primo de Rivera (First Dictatorship) provoked the almost immediate collapse of all that had been achieved. With the disappearance of the *Mancomunitat*, abolished in 1924, an extremely repressive period began that would only end with the dictator's fall in 1930.

There followed a brief transitional period until the municipal elections of April 1931 saw the triumph in Catalonia of the nationalist party *Esquerra Republicana de Catalunya* (Republican Left of Catalonia). The president of its governing council, Francesc Macià, proclaimed the Catalan Republic on 14 April, yet had to renounce that form of government and accept another —guaranteeing autonomy—which was given the historic name of the *Generalitat de Catalunya* and over which Macià presided within the framework of the Second Spanish Republic. Upon his death in December 1933, he was succeeded by Lluís Companys, who was imprisoned in October of the following year. The Statute of Catalan Autonomy was suspended on that date and was not reestablished until February 1936. The Spanish Civil War, however, prelude to the Second World War, broke out in July of the same year. The direct support of the German and Italian totalitarian governments, with the complicity of the English authorities, swamped the Spanish Republic, held in disrepute, moreover, for certain revolutionary excesses.

In February 1939 the whole of Catalonia was occupied by the insurgent forces. The following years witnessed a ruthless repression of various areas of Catalan life, economic, political and cultural.

After the dictator's death in 1975, there followed a transitional period marked by the reestablishment of the monarchy and the ascension to the throne of King Juan Carlos I. In 1977 Josep Tarradellas, elected President of the Generalitat in exile in 1954, was able to return to Barcelona to assume his functions. In 1979 Catalonia received from the Spanish Cortes—and later ratified—a Statute of Autonomy, still in force, but full of ambiguities in its drafting and contradictions in its application. After the first elections to the Parliament of Catalonia, President Tarradellas was succeeded in 1980 by Jordi Pujol, reelected in 1984 and 1988.

Josep Mirabent (1831-1899). Large Vase with Flowers, about 1885 (150 × 102).
Museum of Modern Art, Barcelona.

THEMES AND TECHNIQUES

Before beginning a description of pictorial forms and styles, I shall mention the themes and techniques employed, for they may help us to understand existing differences and how each of the various genres has developed.

Lest we forget, most genres have precedents in earlier periods, although their treatment varied considerably.

FLOWERS AND STILL LIFES

I shall begin with flower painting because it represents an undeniable continuity with the eighteenth century and, more concretely, with a specific discipline established in Barcelona's School of Llotja from its foundation in 1775. In addition to pictures with flowers, alone or combined with figures, flowers play a vital part in the ornamental painting of interiors and in two utilitarian applications, namely as the main theme of silk fabrics, after the French model —a luxury good; or in printing on cotton, the so-called *indianas* (linen or cotton cloths decorated on one side only), a widespread technique in Catalonia during the eighteenth century.

The two most distinguished Catalan artists in each of these applications were Salvador Molet and Carles Ardit. Molet won various prizes in Barcelona between 1791 and 1798, was granted a scholarship to study in Valencia (a silk-making centre modelled on the silk industries of Lyons) and eventually returned to Barcelona where he died in 1836, after having directed instruction in flower painting for many years. The Sant Jordi Academy of Fine Arts boasts a large number of works by this artist and his pupils, among whom we might mention Gabriel Planella, a professor in turn who belonged to a large family of painters, and Francesc Lacoma i Fontanet, a prizewinner from 1799 to 1802 who later settled in Paris, where he died in 1849. He has left us a number of distinguished still lifes of flowers and fruit.

In another direction Carles Ardit, awarded various prizes between 1791 and 1798, obtained a scholarship to study in Switzerland the art of flower painting applied to printed material. Following his return to Barcelona he published a book of a technical nature in 1819.

Towards the middle of the last century, one of the most representative Catalan artists specialized in the painting of flowers, apart from Lacoma, was Francesc Jubany i Carreras (1787-1892). In the second half of that century, the most famous and prolific was Josep Mirabent i Gatell (1831-1899). His son wrote a remarkable description of the artist's working methods, among which the representation of large vases full of flowers from each month stands out. Mirabent i Gatell dedicated one full year to the execution of this series so that he could include flowers from the whole year round painted from life.

The use of flowers forming bouquets and garlands was very common in the decorative painting of bourgeois houses. One of the best-known examples is the decoration of the Barcelona residence of the Garriga Nogués family (1902-1904). Around the same time the most prolific painter in this subject was Aureli Tolosa i Alsina (1861-1938), who executed large compositions, mostly of chrysanthemums, the favourite flower during the modernist period, just as peonies had been until then.

During the twentieth century, flower painting lost its pre-eminent place to the still life, although this did not exclude the near total dedication of some to the genre, Domènec Carles (1888-1962), for instance, a painter who devoted himself to depicting roses, and Hermen Anglada Camarasa who, above all between the years 1930 and 1947, created lavish vases and columns of flowers for obviously decorative ends. By way of contrast, I should mention Ramon Calsina, who often produced singular representations of roses in tin cans. Xavier Nogués occasionally produced some floral compositions of great quality.

Women painters native to Catalonia such as Pepita Teixidor, Maria Rusiñol and Lola Bech have often devoted themselves to the painting of flowers or still lifes, as did women artists who settled in Catalonia, Olga Sacharoff from Georgia and Suzanne Davit from France, for example.

The still life has always persisted, although its popularity has fluctuated over the years. I have already mentioned Lacoma and Jubany. As for Mirabent, I must include one of his specialities, the painting of bunches of grapes, executed in almost hyperrealist detail, which brought him great success in his day. The Museum of the Vine in Vilafranca del Penedès and Barcelona's Museum of Modern Art possess very representative examples of Mirabent's gift.

Hunting themes, a favourite of eighteenth-century painters, were reintroduced in the nineteenth century by Ramon Martí i Alsina (1826-1894) in a realist vein. We find further examples much later and most eloquently in the great compositions of Alfred Sisquella (1900-1964) and Rafael Durancamps (1891-1979), adopting a very different presentation, with the predominant use of artificial light in the latter's case.

Nevertheless, there are other widely differing classes of interpretation, often highly esteemed as well. Firstly, we may mention the still lifes of Isidre Nonell's last period, dating from 1910. We shall find his impasto and the same expressive density in some still lifes by Nicolau Raurich (1871-1945), although they differ in other respects, and even in *Swiss Chard* by Josep Gausachs (1934). Miquel Villà also uses thickly applied paint, although the roundness of his outlines and the strength of his colours set him apart.

Rafael Llimona, Joan Serra, Josep F. Ràfols, Ignasi Mundó and Xavier Valls, among many others, have called upon their sensitivity and good craftmanship to create fine still lifes, demonstrating the various expressive possibilities of this genre.

Magic realism reached a high state of perfection in Feliu Elias' works and up to a point the same can be said of some of Salvador Dalí's paintings, like *The Basket of Bread* (1926). In his extensive œuvre, however, this singular composition is preceded and followed by works of widely varying types, from school works to *Still Life by Moonlight* (1927) with its obvious resonances of the last stage of cubism, to the compositions with limp watches (one of Dalí's oddest inventions) set against landscape backgrounds, as in *The Persistence of Memory* (1931).

At the very opposite end of the scale lie Joan Miró's still lifes, painted mostly between 1915 and 1923 and especially between 1920 and 1929. Miró said in 1928: ". . . What definitely made Picasso more interested in my work was *The Table* . . . Because of this canvas Picasso sent a lot of dealers to me. It was a very dense, disciplined canvas that made it possible to see where my production was going." Still later, though only as an exception, Miró employed a comparable formula, changing his palette, however, in the dramatic still life showing a pair of old shoes, painted while his thoughts were haunted with the Spanish Civil War.

In this genre, as in so many others, Picasso combined within himself most of the forms and idioms common to these other artists. The still life, together with the human figure, always played a preponderant role in his production and throughout each stage of his artistic expression, especially in the Blue Period and the various forms and chromatic ranges of cubism.

LANDSCAPE

During the late baroque and neoclassical periods landscape painting, including landscapes used in the theatre for scene painting, seems to have been common in Catalonia. This continued without interruption down to the beginning of the nineteenth century. Artists and scene painters carrying out decorative functions had plenty to do but were often relegated to a secondary role, as if their work were a complement to painting proper.

Views and landscapes often included ruined buildings, after a picturesque formula preserved throughout the Romantic period.

One of the most representative artists of this dual vocation was Pau Rigalt, born in Barcelona in 1778 and died in that city in 1845. In 1816 he was appointed painter of the Santa Creu Theatre (as Manuel Tramulles had been previously) and in 1825 the Chamber of Commerce nominated him director of the perspective and landscape class, a post to which his son Lluís succeeded. In addition to numerous mural decorations, Pau painted sixteen landscapes in oils for the Chamber. Lluís often worked from life, but we know that he also used French lithographs with examples of different species of trees.

Lluís Rigalt (1814-1894). Montserrat Mountain (43 × 57).
Museum of Modern Art, Barcelona.

Lluís Rigalt, with his paintings and innumerable drawings, is one of the best representatives of Romantic landscape painting in Catalonia, although many other contemporary painters were active, Xavier Parcerisa (1803-1876) for example, who illustrated the volumes of *Memories and Beauties of Spain*, which include a total of 588 lithographs, and turned out a number of large canvases, among which the Alcázar of Seville has preserved two fine works representing the interior of Sant Pere de Rodes and Barcelona Cathedral.

The artistic atmosphere surrounding these painters is comparable to that prevading French Romantic illustrations, running from the works of Baron Taylor to those of Langlois and Gustave Doré. Scene painting was of particular importance and established a prolific Catalan school which has lasted until the twentieth century.

In 1851 the painter Josep Galofre published a professional guide bearing a very suggestive title, *The artist in Italy and other European countries in view of the present state of the Fine Arts*. The following fragments come from Chapter 15, mainly devoted to landscape painting:

"Undoubtedly the landscape, so widely accepted in our society which loves the countryside for fashionable reasons or of necessity, not only has not interrupted the admirable progress of the artists of 1600, but also, within the large group of artists who cultivate it today, there are some who have surpassed, in my opinion, many of their ancient forerunners; as has also happened, we shall see, with genre painting.

"Today we have landscape painters of such skill, knowledge and dash that they will create an epoch in art and will rival in the future the classics already mentioned, once fame has made their names universally known. To some, this eulogy will appear exaggerated, but I call on time to prove me right. Yes, the modern landscape painter has found both in *choice* and *execution* unhoped-for secrets and the proof lies in those magnificent sunsets, those warm tones of Naples and Palermo, and indeed the profusion of views that the ancients knew nothing of, India, America, Africa, Occeania [*sic*], China and the North. The moderns have left us nothing they have not depicted; there is scarcely a single corner they have not reproduced.

"... Then, as he finds himself capable of seeing nature and transferring its wonderful effects to his imagination, he will begin to make a good collection of studies or fragments painted on a folded sheet of prepared paper, a practice that helps to choose the best point and the best moment of the picturesque effect. In this way, then, I shall divide the studies into various classes, as follows:

"Firstly. The *air*, or atmosphere, copying it at different hours of the day, especially at sunrise and sunset, when the tints are so fine, so delicate and in harmony; for it is of little interest from nine in the morning until three or five o'clock in the afternoon in summer, because of the excess light which prevents the fine perception of colouring and chiaroscuro in the best viewpoints. The beautiful and varied clouds that appear in the hours immediately following the rising and setting of the life-giving star, with a thousand unexpected effects of light and colour (discarding those which do not seem of interest to the Artist and copying those appropriate to his taste and feelings), form a large part of the study of landscape.

"Secondly. *Mountains*, be they high or low, afford another interesting object, with so much beauty of outline as the nature of southern Europe offers, that they enchant and surprise the intelligent observer. In this sphere our Spain, in several of its provinces, remains unrivalled, not even by southern Italy which is so beautiful and picturesque.

"Sicily offers divine studies of mountains, which are of a thousand shades of violet at sunrise and sunset. During the winter of 1848 I spent two months in Naples and Vesuvius, and the nearby mountains presented each hour, each minute, a truly marvellous picture. The upper part of Vesuvius was covered with snow and at sunset—and even earlier—despite our being in the month of January, it looked golden as on summer days, and the skirt of the mountain looked so purple that mixed tints of carmine and cobalt might emerge. The mountains in the background, with a magnificent outline, were crowned with the beautiful blue of the sea, one of the most surprising spectacles of nature that I have seen in my life and which I should never tire of looking at.

"All the Apennines offer many degrees of interest to the observant landscape painter. The environs of Perugia and Lake Trasimeno; the viewpoint to be seen on leaving Aquapendente for Tuscany; those existing around Florence and the many offered during the journey from Pisa to Genoa provide material for perfecting oneself in the enjoyable study of mountains. Furthermore, the Alps that appear between Turin and Milan, rising up as if by magic around the former of those cities, as well as lakes Como and Maggiore, constantly afford the observant landscape painter an object worthy of his meditations, both for the different tones of purple on the lower slopes, and for the snow on the heights, formed by an outline rich and varied, capricious and original. If you cross Mount Stelvio under twelve feet of snow and descend on the Tyrolean side, you can also admire a new and picturesque nature, already very different from the beautiful and enchanting nature of Switzerland, whose main points are so well known and described that they require no mention here.

"Thirdly. *Trees* form another of landscape painters' special studies, needing a particular intelligence to understand them. The famous *Claude* was wonderful in his and serves as a standard for modern painters. So the Artist should pay special attention when studying them, because excellent landscape painters, who understand the *air* and the *mountains* well, at times do not know how to compose *trees* properly. Consequently, pick out good groups from nature, with various qualities and tones, taking care that they are well portrayed, when nature presents herself in all her beauty and luxuriance.

"Italy is not always as rich in grandiose rural woods, as it is in gardens and country houses; our Spain is, generally speaking, even less so in both of these. Nevertheless, I remember having seen fertile examples of the former in Sicily and around Roman *villas*, and in the environs of Albano, where there is a famous park belonging to Prince Chigi, which has been abandoned for fifty years to the simple forces of nature. I have also observed some beautiful groups on the outskirts of Florence and Milan. If the trees of Versailles and Fontainebleau, the English parks and the Granja could be gilded with the sunny tints of Naples and Palermo, together they would form the most sublime effect that could be desired in this sphere, so interesting to the landscape painter. Those of the Alhambra are without parallel anywhere.

"Fourthly. The *foreground* is another of the most interesting points of the landscape, and as such, requires detailed study. A road covered with thousands of pebbles, bushes, grass and rocks, along which lies a half-broken-down wall with a thousand branches crowning and concealing it, with ivy here, a plant there, a rivulet that winds through this road forming a thousand different tints and moves towards the plain; in short, everything contributes to the splendour of the work, the completeness of the picture after the painter arranges it to his own taste.

"Once the Artist has a good collection of studies and fragments in this form, once he knows and has a good understanding of the *air*, *mountains*, *trees* and the *foreground*, he may attempt the *composition*; that is to say do what I have said when speaking of beauty; trace an outline that is taken from nature in its constituent parts and which we could hardly find assembled in nature. To this end, I shall make the following comment:

"Let us suppose that one has to paint the marvellous panorama of Naples, seen from Posillipo, from a point whence the city, Vesuvius and the background produce a good effect, but whose foreground lacks interest. Then one will make a study, for this foreground alone, so that it has local character, and the painter will apply it to the general viewpoint to form the unity of work, to which end trees are sometimes added, houses removed and the sky improved; which, without harming the exactitude of the original, perfects it in its ideal beauty, the painter presenting it as more beautiful than what the observer saw in that same nature."

Tomàs Moragas (1837-1906). Moroccan Scene (48 × 70).
Museum of Modern Art, Barcelona.

The fact is that their owners are civilized and understand that they should be preserved; they are jewels of the tradition. All that was beautiful. The whole district of Olot was covered with century-old trees and the interior of these woods seemed like a cathedral, such was the majestic silence and sense of well-being that one found there.

". . . That Pla de Llacs and that Fluvià have disappeared. How that river moved me! How delicious was the mystery of those islets amidst those fallen poplars, which were mirrored there

In fact, these concepts are applicable to the pictorial naturalism prevailing for many years and I would say that it still exists today in the case of a large number of painters. In 1862 the Majorcan Joan O'Neille i Rosiñol (1828-1907) published a *Treatise on Landscape* which has little new to contribute, yet retains our interest as the first monographic manual to appear in our region. In addition to general themes, it alludes to the cycles of the four seasons and how light varies depending on whether it is morning, noon, afternoon or night.

For all that, there existed obvious signs of development. An example in Catalan landscape painting is Ramon Martí i Alsina (1826-1894) who, in landscapes and, as much or even more, in seascapes, stimulated the production and appreciation of the genre, creating a master in and

Eliseu Meifrèn (1859-1940). Cadaqués Landscape (52 × 64).
Private collection.

as if reflected in that water so rich in colours. Before the little bridge leading to Santa Pau existed, one crossed by a footbridge; in the direction of Santa Magdalena, to the right, a slope led to Prat de les Móres, a centre of infinite delights; and further to the right those fields of corn in June and those famous terraces in September were like rich carpets for entering the town. And at dusk, loving couples were always passing along the roads, as was that little flock of sheep that used to move along the solitary paths in the evening. In the distance, in summer, one heard the *tenora* softly sounding from Sant Roc or la Xatona, filling the heart with joy. What unforgettable times! How different from today! How sweet life was! La Fageda d'en Jordà, one could see it almost whole. I still possess studies of tall beech trees, the remains of what was felled following the Carlist war; then it did not turn out as damaged as the last time; now nothing remains of what there was. That was a temple for peaceful meditation; that quiet touched the heart; from that velvety rock-strewn place rose columns like bright green marble, speckled with yellow moss; and from the branches of the beech trees grew those leaves that the lightest of breezes would flutter continuously.''

Modest Urgell (1839-1919), evincing a more poetic and literary personality, worked in Barcelona and the Empordà, and established contacts with the Olot group.

Olot landscape painting has continued to the present, down many generations. This is proved, among many others, by Francesc Vayreda, Pere Gussinyé, Barnadas, Gelabert, Maurici Vallsquer and other artists who settled in Olot, Iu Pascual and Josep Pujol, for example.

In the Empordà, Marian Llavanera, Ramon Reig and Frederic Lloveras (with a much wider sphere of activity) worked along similar lines; Ignasi Mallol (1892-1940), a native of Tarragon, is another outstanding figure.

Nevertheless, before continuing I must mention that along with the Olot group, there existed in the late nineteenth century in Catalonia a group of luminist painters with roots in Rome, Naples and Venice, who settled in various centres on the Catalan coast, especially in Cadaqués, Blanes and Sitges. Among the most important are Eliseu Meifrèn (1859-1940), Joan Roig i Soler (1852-1909) and Arcadi Mas i Fondevila (1852-1934), not to mention the contributions of local artists. Ten years later, painters such as Joan Llimona (1860-1926) and Dionís Baixeras (1862-1943) continued to cultivate a balanced naturalism. The change was to come by way of Paris, thanks to the impact of the great international exhibitions of painting, to which was added, beginning in 1888, the Barcelona show, repeated between 1891 and 1911. Besides the impressionist interpretation of landscape, with pure and luminous colours, there were artists devoted to symbolism and a grey atmosphere, more reminiscent of Whistler's palette.

This lyrical and poetic vision, however, together with the luminist tradition boasted but two distinguished Catalan practitioners, Ramon Casas (1866-1932), throughout his Parisian period, and Santiago Rusiñol (1861-1931). This was the art called *modernista*, a term I shall study in more detail in one of the following chapters.

In 1883 Fontanals del Castillo stated that painting in Barcelona advanced by decades, yet the fact remains that the painters born in the 70s, Hermen Anglada, Joaquim Mir, Isidre Nonell, Xavier Nogués, Ricard Canals, Joaquim Sunyer, Marian Pidelaserra, Pere Torné Esquius and Joan Colom among others, were active in different and very varied fields.

Some subscribed to a late impressionism, as was the case with Joaquim Sunyer in the first years of his career, Joan Colom and Pere Ysern i Alié (1875-1946).

Pidelaserra was attracted to pointillism, as described by Francesc Pujols when referring to the paintings executed in 1903,

Marian Pidelaserra (1877-1946). A Mountain, Montseny, the Setting Sun, about 1903 (79 × 89).
Museum of Modern Art, Barcelona.

"The paintings of Montseny . . . were based on pointillism, the technique that, while preserving—even increasing—the concreteness of vision, also preserved the diluted atmosphere of objects dissolved in air and light . . .

"In his early days, Pidelaserra would become a pointillist, like the spring which, being the first season of the year after winter, which is pure line, details and specifies everything with tree leaves . . . A spring landscape is always a pointillist landscape . . . Afterwards, with the approach of summer, the brushstrokes of spring begin to thicken and melt into each other . . . When his vision passes from spring to summer, like the visions of nature . . ."

Joaquim Mir, following a period during which he showed himself dependent still on the Olot school and Mas i Fondevilla, would embark on a lively and decorative colourism that would embrace two of his most personal periods, that of Majorca (1901-1904) and the Tarragona countryside, wherein bright and soft colours are diversified into multicoloured patches .

Hermen Anglada would borrow the language of academicism and impressionism in the early phase of his painting, before moving on to a decorativism comparable to Picasso's and Van Dongen's. Later, this virtuoso and attractive decorativism, mentioned above when dealing with flowers, was to persist until the last years of his production and his underwater seascapes—one of the most personal features characterizing this period—which appear much more realistic than one might imagine although combined with sirens and other fantastic elements.

Hermen Anglada Camarasa (1871-1959). Siren, 1927-1928 (210 × 200).
Private collection.

Pere Torné Esquius (1879-1936). Drawing-Room Interior, about 1910 (40 × 48).
Museum of Modern Art, Barcelona.

Pere Torné Esquius (1879-1936), with a special gift for intimate atmosphere and a delicate palette that recalls certain French Nabis, gave rise to this very personal commentary by Joan Maragall. A poet though no art critic, Maragall, in his presentation of *Beautiful Places in Catalonia* (published in 1910), praised pictorial intimism:

"It is the feeling for the lines of the humblest things, insignificant when they are not looked at with love: . . . what the folds of a curtain half drawn in front of a window say and the attraction of an open door and the mystery of a closed door; what the carefully aligned flowerpots on a patio bench mean, or a rose branch climbing like a garland around the niche containing a Christ signifies; the repose offered by a vase of flowers on a table in a room; the clock on the wall and the cat curled up asleep on a chair, the sadness of the rocking-chair abandoned in the middle of a little garden and . . . here there is the delight of the novelty we find in this representation of so many old things . . . but with an inexhaustible sense, eternal as everything created, new each time in the personal eyes of each artist."

Jaume Mercadé (1887-1967) and Josep Mompou (1888-1968) are often called *Fauves*, though we should remember that their so-called "ferocity" is something closer to the colours and forms of Albert Marquet than to those of other French artists. Two of these, Henri Matisse and Raoul Dufy, stayed a short while in the Roussillon and the latter also spent some time in the Vallès, in the vicinity of his friend Manolo Hugué (1872-1945).

The second phase marking Joaquim Sunyer's art, centred on Majorca, Ceret and Sitges, abounds with resonances of Cézanne at a time when Derain and Picasso were working in Catalonia and the latter, after Barcelona and Gósol, was creating cubist art jointly with Braque.

Very soon afterwards, Joan Miró painted his landscapes of the Tarragona countryside during two periods that are reflected in his correspondence with the Vilanova painters Enric C. Ricart and Josep F. Ràfols. I have taken the following paragraphs from the letters he sent them:

". . . This summer [1917] I have worked hard and visited many towns and mountains . . . A very sad, but striking consequence is to see that a man remains the same whether he lives in a landscape, town or mountain . . . and whether he speeds over a landscape in which everything is a lyricism of colour . . . Everything moves him equally, he talks in the same way and is the same, and paints the same; with the same emotion as he would paint Majorca, let us say, he paints Toledo, varying only what the *photographic* material has to offer . . . The opposite man is he who sees a different problem in every tree and every stretch of country; this is the man who suffers, the one who is forever on the move, can never sit down, he who will never execute what people call a definitive work, he is the man who is always stumbling and always picking himself up again . . .

"For the moment [1918] what interests me most is the calligraphy of a tree or a tiled roof, leaf by leaf, branch by branch, grass by grass, tile by tile . . .

"You'll see that I'm very slow with my work. With the time I spend working on a canvas, I start loving it. Love born of a slow understanding. A slow understanding because of the great wealth of—concentrated—nuances that the sun provides.

"I enjoy coming to understand a clump of grass in a landscape. Why look down on it? A bit of grass is as charming as a tree or a mountain.

"Except for the primitives and the Japanese, nearly everyone leaves it aside, an object that is so heavenly.

"They all seek out and paint the great masses of trees or mountains, not hearing the music of the grasses and the little flowers, and without valuing the little stones in a narrow gully, gratuitously."

It is worthwhile contrasting these declarations with those made by Joaquim Vayreda in a letter to Carles Pirozzini dated 1885 that has already been transcribed. But let us continue with Miró's text,

"I am still working on the canvas of the village [Mont-roig] and am executing another large one, the landscape of olive and carob trees and vines to be seen from my room . . . With these two canvases it seems that I shall work for the whole summer . . . I don't known how I shall finish the picture with the olive trees, it began cubist and now it has turned pointillist."

And in 1923 he wrote,

"This year I am making a determined attack on the landscape and, to relax, still lifes. I have already succeeded in completely divesting myself of nature, and the landscapes have nothing to do with external reality. Nevertheless, they have more of *Mont-roig* in them than if they were executed *d'après nature*.

"I always work at home and have only nature to consult . . ."

While Miró was following his pictorial itinerary, Salvador Dalí (1904-1989) was undertaking his own around 1926, after a period of experimentation. His concept of landscape was very different and always three-dimensional. I have already mentioned this concept when discussing his still lifes, in which landscape backgrounds are nearly always present, especially from 1926 onwards. The basis is often Portlligat or the beach of Roses on the northern coast of Catalonia. The rocks of Cape Creus provided him with features that, on appearance, might be volcanic or lunar but in fact are the product of wind erosion. Their character stems from the works of German symbolists such as Arnold Böcklin, although these compositions develop towards a personal, hallucinatory world.

Dalí wrote many autobiographical texts; I take the following fragment from one of them, written with André Parinaud in 1973,

"When we were children, my father used to take us for a walk to Cape Creus. I need only to close my eyes to relive, untouched, those landscapes, those images, and then I set up the strangest of dialogues with myself. All the rocks, all the hills of Cape Creus, are in a permanent state of metamorphosis. Each one of them is in a permanent metamorphosis. Each one is a suggestion that enables me spontaneously to imagine an eagle, a horse, a cock, a lion, a woman . . . Yet if we reached the sea, as we drew near, the symbolism did not cease to develop, to be transformed. . . On this cape dedicated to Aphrodite by the ancients, the tramontana has sculptured dream figures just as I model the figures in the theatre of my life. In order to hear my secret voice, I must first have listened for a long time to the song of the wind on the point of the Pyrenean rocks . . . This cape, the extremity of Catalonia, is one of the sublime places where the sacred spirit gives nourishment: the background waves that come from the depths of the sea join up with the gust of wind that descends from the heavens to fertilize our land.''

We should not forget, however, that at the same time hundreds of artists were painting thousands of landscapes of a totally conservative type. Much later, at the end of the Second World War, a group of artists of widely different origins banded together under the influence of the review *Dau al Set* (*Dice at Seven*), to experiment with the painting of fantastic landscapes. Some, such as Joan Ponç (1927-1984), would remain faithful to this trend. For others, however, such as Antoni Tàpies (1923), Modest Cuixart (1925) and Joan-Josep Tharrats (1918), this period (explicitly inspired by their acquaintance with the work of Paul Klee) was to be much shorter, although interesting nonetheless.

After the death of Joan Ponç, many landscape painters remained faithful or returned to the more traditional formulas, while others moved on to informalism or expressed themselves by means of a new intimism, as in the case of Xavier Valls or (in his last period) Francesc Todó.

FIGURE PAINTING

Setting aside portraits and compositions with figures that have no specific meaning, I shall begin this section with painting that employs mythological themes.

Training at the art academies around 1800 remained faithful to neoclassical models, among which those founded on Greco-Roman themes predominated. This explains why artists who went to study in Rome, including Fortuny (his *Nereids* of 1857 and *Bacchant* of 1858), made use of this repertory, although Fortuny's own inclinations, for example, ran in quite a different direction.

Sporadically, much later painters, such as Aleix Clapés (1850-1920), a collaborator of Gaudí's, executed works with mythological themes on commission. Clapés, for example, was paid to illustrate passages from *Atlantis*, a poem by Jacint Verdaguer.

The growing predominance of history and genre painting led to the progressive disappearance of mythological themes until, in the early twentieth century, they reappeared as mural painters rediscovered the classical world in their work. This began in Catalonia with the creative production of Joaquim Torres Garcia, who abandoned modernism and naturalism to make his first journey to Italy (1911) in order to prepare the decoration of the Hall of St George in the Palace of the *Generalitat* of Catalonia in Barcelona. The immediate consequences of Garcia's change were his paintings of Terrassa and the emergence in Sarrià, under his teaching, of a school of decoration. Josep Obiols, for one, joined the school and Francesc d'Assís Galí was associated with it.

Ideologically, it is worth mentioning that in his book of poems *Italy* (1918) Josep Aragay proposed an improbable synthesis between Cézanne's apples and the Roman splendours reminiscent of Giorgio de Chirico,

"I should like to know how to paint an apple really well,
not forgetting, for all that, the majesty of Rome."

In his hands and those of other artists, the classical world persisted in the work of certain painters, although it would have to wait until 1925 to acquire a new impulse thanks to some of Salvador Dali''s compositions, often combined with the landscapes he loved so much. Later, his obsession with Gala, his wife, would be varied in themes that are only superficially mythological or religious (*Atomic Leda* and *The Madonna of Portlligat*).

Joan Llimona (1860-1926).
Detail of the decorations adorning a chapel dome, Montserrat Monastery church.

Painting with religious themes depended more on commissions received by artists than on an ideological basis. That does not mean to say, however, that in certain noteworthy examples no such basis existed. In the early nineteenth century, the first artist we should mention is Josep Flaugier. Later we should single out the œuvre of three Catalan artists who established contacts in Rome with the Nazarenes, a mystical group of Germans and Italians that was founded there. Pau Milà i Fontanals (1810-1883) and Claudi Lorenzale (1814-1889) were the most fervent adherents of this group, though there were others too, such as Josep Arrau i Barba (1802-1872) and Pelegrí Clavé (1811-1880). The culminating phase of their stay in Italy is centred on the years 1832-1841. On their return, the academic chairs of Milà and Lorenzale in Barcelona allowed the doctrines they had assimilated to reach a vast audience. They greatly influenced Marian Fortuny during the years of his training as an artist, seen in works such as *St Paul on the Areopagus*.

The Roussillon painter Jaume Llantà (1807-1864) presented various pictures with religious themes at the Paris Salons. They included a theme of devotion to the sanctuary of Núria in 1838 and ten years later, a work entitled *It is Faith that Saves*.

A solid academic training enabled Benet Mercadé to paint large compositions such as *The Transfer of the Mortal Remains of St Francis of Assisi* (Paris Salon, 1866) and *St Teresa* (1869).

The Barcelona tradition lasted much longer thanks to mural painters such as Eduard Llorens (1838-1913) and Victorià Codina Langlin (1844-1911), who settled in London for many years; Langlin achieved great fame for his decoration of the dome of the Basilica de la Mercè in Barcelona as well as the execution of large paintings on cloth imitating tapestries (Pedralbes Monastery, etc.).

An interesting phenomenon in Barcelona was the creation, in 1893, of a confessional group of Catholic artists, the Cercle Artístic de Sant Lluc (Artistic Circle of St Luke) in which the Llimona brothers, Joan, a painter (1860-1926), and Josep, a sculptor, would distinguish themselves. Others who belonged to the Cercle in its initial phase were Alexandre de Riquer (1856-1920), Dionís Baixeras (1862-1943) and Juli Gonzàlez, and later on, Darius Vilàs (1880-1950). The group's ideological mentor was Josep Torras i Bages (1846-1916), who was consecrated bishop of Vic in 1899.

Alexandre de Riquer carried out the monumental pictorial decoration of the Montserrat Monastery church; Dionís Baixeras and Josep Maria Tamburini painted great canvases on religious themes there; Joan Llimona decorated the dome of Montserrat's Chamber of the Virgin and the baldaquin of Ripoll Monastery.

Nevertheless, the most spectacular commission was undoubtedly the decoration of Vic Cathedral. In 1900 Josep Maria Sert (1874-1945) wrote to Dr Torras i Bages asking him for the opportunity to decorate a church in his diocese. As a result Sert was commissioned, the bishop offering him Vic Cathedral. Sert set to work with a great sense of responsibility. He made several initial life-size studies in oils and full colour, later executed a number of others in blue and black on a silver ground and finally decided on a sepia tone on a gold ground. After the preliminary work on sketches and the definitive realization of the decorations—completed only in 1930—the edifice was destroyed by fire and Sert began new decorations, executed between 1940 and 1945, with few innovations.

Picasso maintained friendly ties with the Cercle and as late as 1959 participated in a public homage to the group, to which Joan Miró also contributed. The latter executed the illustrations for *The Canticle of the Sun* by St Francis, but ultimately was unable to carry out the mural decorations planned for the Chapel of the Annunciation in Sant Vicenç de Sarrià, for which the poet Josep Vicenç Foix had suggested that he be commissioned.

The group's mentors later included, among others, Dr Manuel Trens (1892-1976) and Father Jordi Llimona (1924), son of the painter Rafael Llimona (1896-1957), who was Joan's nephew.

We might mention the names of other artists active either inside or outside the Cercle de Sant Lluc in successive stages throughout the twentieth century, Joaquim Torres Garcia (parish church of Sant Augustí in Barcelona and the Divina Pastora Convent in Sarrià), Antoni Vila Arrufat (1894-1989), with important commissions in Terrassa, Sabadell and Sant Sebastià de

in Madrid in 1864 an episode of the Mexican War, in which General Prim participated, just as he would participate in the Moroccan campaign.

Montmajor, Joan Commeleran (1902), Pere Pruna (1904-1977), Jaume Busquets, Joaquim Ros (1906-1991), Montserrat Casanova (1909-1991), Ramon Rogent (1920-1958), Domènec Fita (1927) and in particular Josep Obiols (1894-1967), author (among other works) of many mural paintings in Montserrat Monastery (sacristy, a reliquary chapel, etc.).

In addition to the abundance of works with more or less religious themes by Salvador Dalí

The Carlist wars were the chosen theme (though from opposing points of view in the conflict) of the soldier Josep Cusachs (1851-1908) on the one hand, and the brothers Joaquim and Marian Vayreda on the other. The latter played, moreover, quite an important role in those wars.

Josep-Lluís Pellicer has left us a testimony of revolutionary Rome in his work *Zitto, silenzio, che passa la ronda* (1869). The year 1875 saw the painter in Arabistan (the Iranian region of Abadan, near the Persian Gulf), where he painted a great composition which he exhibited at the Paris Salon of 1878. He subsequently took part as graphic chronicler in the Russo-Turkish War (1877-1878)—his illustrations of Bulgaria are documents of the first rank—and in the last Carlist war.

The Universal Exhibition of Barcelona in 1888 gave rise to paintings that varied greatly in character. Later, social themes predominated, mainly represented by the painters Joan Planella (1850-1910), Lluís Graner (1863-1929), Antoni Serra i Fiter (1869-1932), Ramon Casas, with two versions of the general strike of 1902, Joaquim Torres Garcia and Marian Pidelaserra, the latter with the disturbing series *The Conquered*, a pictorial evocation painted from memory of the different aspects of human misery.

History painting had a much more limited scope in the twentieth century, if we except some important groups by Josep Maria Sert, for example the decoration of the Hall of the Chronicles in Barcelona's town hall, and the paintings in the Maricel Palace at Sitges, with allegories of the First World War. Also worth mentioning are the excellent studies by Oleguer Junyent, Francesc Labarta, Ricard Canals, Francesc d'A. Galí and Xavier Nogués for the execution of some dioramas in the National Palace of the Exhibition of 1929. Apart from those, I can only mention some notable, albeit sporadic, examples, *The Barcelona Strike* (1930) by Ramon Calsina; *The Reaper* (1937) by Joan Miró; the great ceiling by Martí Bas depicting the Badajoz assassinations (1937); and a composition by Francesc García Vilella on the so-called *tramway* strike in Barcelona, dating from 1951. Lastly, in a world much closer to symbolism, we might mention several of the Spanish Civil War posters.

In more recent compositions, Josep Guinovart and Antoni Tàpies have resorted to an emblematic idiom.

There are widely varying examples of genre painting which we shall cover in chapters to come. Yet almost the only outstanding works are those by Marian Fortuny, Simó Gómez (1845-1880) and Francesc Miralles (1848-1901), as well as some groups by Josep Maria Sert. Sert also proved extraordinarily productive within the scope of his permanent preoccupation with the baroque.

With these few examples we might associate works of an often symbolic and decorative nature, especially those by Xavier Nogués, Josep Aragay and Josep Obiols.

Josep Maria Sert (1874-1945). The Epic of Catalans in the East. The Avalanche, about 1929.
Detail of the decorations of the Hall of the Chronicles, Town Hall, Barcelona.

HISTORICAL STAGES AND ARTISTIC LANGUAGE

From this point on, I shall do my best to develop my account in a continuous thread. However, I shall not be able to confine myself to a strictly chronological development, given I shall have to bear in mind many parallel artistic careers and the occasional partial or total involvement with a particular concept.

Nevertheless, we must consider the conventional—though very useful—labels, the so-called *isms* that the critics have often claimed to identify with a *chemically pure* uniformity, a concept that is usually incompatible with the more or less real freedom of artistic creation. The demythicizing fashions of recent years (with eighteenth-century precedents in the field of historical criticism or hypercriticism, to be sure) have reached a point where critics seek to deny the reality of modernism in the name of this alleged uniformity, which is nonexistent except in extreme cases, such as the beginnings of Picasso's and Braque's cubist production.

Two major difficulties also arise: on the one hand, the inadequate definition of the makeup of human—often ephemeral—groups formed by bonds of friendship far more than by any ideological or aesthetic affinity; and on the other, the problems arising from the use of a vocabulary that may be valid within a limited geographical area, but which presents great difficulties when it has to be translated and consequently understood elsewhere.

One of the first attempts at classification was proposed by Eugeni d'Ors in 1923 at the request of the Barcelona collector Lluís Plandiura. He established four main *hours* (not watertight compartments, but major moments) based on the difference between centres that were dynamic and those where artists congregated: the Llotja, the Sala Parés, Els Quatre Gats and the Plandiura collection. I believe that this criterion holds for the first three cases and is explicable in the fourth for circumstantial and personal reasons, given that on the elimination of the *Mancomunitat* by the First Dictatorship, the artists who represented it were welcomed in part by the above-mentioned collector. This classification is valid for Barcelona and certain specific tastes, but less so as regards the idioms of artistic creation. The nearer we approach the second half of the twentieth century, the more difficult it proves to achieve a relatively critical perspective, especially if we claim to form firmly based judgments.

Once I have analyzed the various systems employed, and without underrating the interest of any of them, I shall try to conform to a formula that is both sound and balanced, and yet remains intelligible to anyone lacking a profound knowledge of Catalan art. At the same time, however, I shall try to avoid the facile, often deceptive, system of proceeding by over-simplified analogies.

Generally speaking, the nineteenth century will be divided into three great periods, namely neoclassicism, Romanticism and realism-naturalism. I shall focus the transition from the nineteenth to the twentieth century on modernism while underscoring all the exceptions—conservative and avant-garde—that parallel this movement. As for the twentieth century, I shall have to work in more or less intercommunicating compartments, tracing, on the one hand, the line that runs from cubism to dadaism, surrealism, informalism and conceptual art; and on the other, the line considered as more conventional which, starting from postmodernism—an expression that remains confusingly defined—passes through *Art Deco* (with certain links with *noucentism*) to arrive at fauvism and expressionism. After the violent rupture in 1939, I shall mention the persistence or return of a more commercial painting, similar to the *pompier* art of France and frequently included in the more generic vision known as *academic* art, a term used in an unfortunately pejorative sense. Side by side with these academic practitioners, I shall treat the permanence of portrait and landscape painting, especially that with its origins in Olot, and the skilful art of watercolourists. I shall exclude other idioms, such as "primitive" or naive art, difficult to group with any of the previously mentioned trends.

Neoclassicism was the reigning norm in the Barcelona school of Llotja from its foundation in 1775. In 1810 Joan Carles Anglès, painter and member of the Chamber of Commerce, praised

". . . the great revolution that has regenerated the arts and produced such beautiful effects in the short space of the preceding thirty years . . . Consequently, Antiquity is the model retained by those who, in honour of the Arts, have undertaken its restoration. Antiquity is that which has trained a Mengs, a David, a Camuccini, a Canova. Antiquity alone can teach the young to philosophize and turn them into erudite members of their profession."

In other documents, Anglès mentions Winckelmann and describes an object of *Ideal Beauty*,

"A head illuminated by the sun at the twilight hour will achieve a most beautiful effect, because the part illuminated by the sun will be tinted by its red colour, the half tones will appear extremely transparent and fiery, and the reflections of the part in the shadows will be illuminated by the universal light of the air, and being blue, the reflections will also be blue."

When Anglès died in 1822, a follower of his, the Romantic writer Ramon López Soler, recalled the studies of Greek and Latin "that opened the gates of ancient mythology to him and made him familiar with Homer, the father of artists. Anglès, aloof from men, moved through the happy centuries of the arts and picked the flowers in the enchanted garden of Poetry; his imagination, noble by nature, was fired by these ideas . . . Nature manifests as well the artist's profound knowledge. It has been copied in neither our century nor our climes; there is some indefinable hint of poetry and enchantment about it, a taste of antiquity that magically transports us to the fabulous world where the scene is represented and artfully contributes to our delight . . ."

Another follower, the painter and chemist Josep Arrau i Barba, also recalling Anglès' pictures, has this to say,

"Although he followed the same maxims as the idealist school, he knew how to stick to Nature better than the other painters of his day."

Arrau counted Josep Flaugier among the Catalans, feeling he could be considered as a native because of his lengthy stay in Barcelona, and qualified the artist as "head of another group of painters whose style seems more conventional than authentic, son of the maxims accepted during the last third of the past century and which have not been completely abandoned unfortunately, maxims recommending the search for ideal beauty in the fantastic realms of the imagination and not in Nature, which offers so many models of true beauty, as mother and depositary of all things good and beautiful."

The coldest and most perfect neoclassicism is found in Flaugier's paintings in the Barcelona Church of Sant Vicenç and Sant Carles Borromeu, whereas a self-portrait in the History Museum of the City of Barcelona and two sketches depicting episodes of the French War (Military Museum of the Castell de Montjuïc) are much less conventional.

When dealing with flower painting in the chapter on themes, I have already mentioned the main Barcelona representatives of this genre, an almost unbroken succession stretching from the end of the eighteenth until well into the nineteenth century. Outstanding in this line are the Molets and Planellas, until we come to Josep Mirabent, medallist in Madrid in 1860 and 1867 and decorated in 1871. He exhibited at the Paris Salons and Universal Exhibitions in 1855, 1863, 1867, 1877 and 1899, often alternating between flowers and his pictures of grapes.

Pelegrí Clavé's first works, a self-portrait in the Barcelona Museum of Modern Art for example, are still obviously Romantic, although later he painted a more academic type of portrait that won him great praise in Mexico, where he also executed landscapes and great compositions with religious themes, such as the decoration of the dome of La Profesa, an ancient Jesuit church (1859-1860). From a conversation *à trois* held around 1860 and recorded in his *Dialogue on the History of Painting in Mexico*, José Bernardo Couto recalls the following remarks by Clavé,

"I did not find a good school or indeed any school in Mexico, and began to teach my pupils from what I had learnt in Barcelona and Rome and the principles that might have trained me through my own observations and talks with skilful artists during my travels in Italy, Spain and France. Among them I shall never forget the distinguished and memorable Overbeck, one

Pelegrí Clavé (1811-1880). Self-Portrait, about 1835 (57 × 47).
Museum of Modern Art, Barcelona.

of the creators of the German school and perhaps the first to initiate the reaction against the profaners of the Renaissance.''

Within the general panorama of Romanticism, Claudi Lorenzale and Pau Milà i Fontanals form a group set apart by its religious themes and its personal relations with the Nazarenes, who were mainly based in Rome, although some were also active in Germany and Austria—indeed the school was actually founded in Vienna—whence certain members hailed (Cornelius, Overbeck). In Italy they were joined by Joaquim Espalter, a native of Sitges specialized in portraits and compositions with figures, and the very prolific miniaturist Lluís Vermell, who painted thousands of portraits and travelled throughout Italy and Catalonia.

Lorenzale and Milà concentrated their activity on teaching in Barcelona, which they did officially from 1843 and 1851 respectively, positions that ensured their reputation was widely diffused and secured them many close personal relations. Upon their return to Barcelona, they continued to take an interest in what was being created outside our country while their own efforts earned them recognition and appreciation beyond our frontiers. We have proof of their

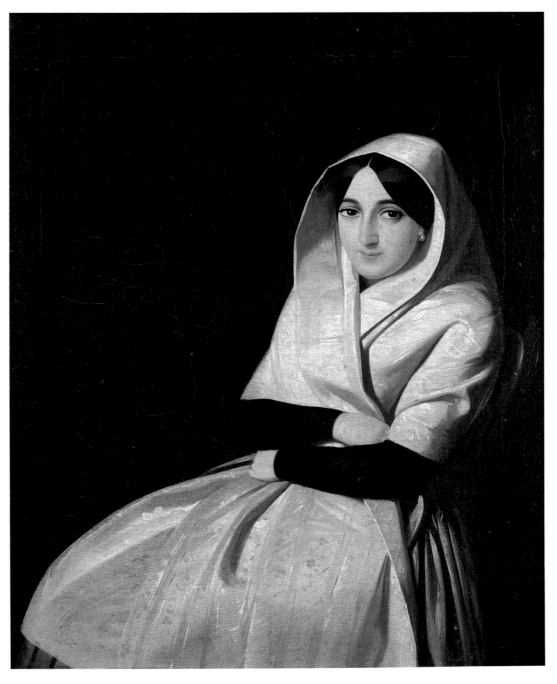

Claudi Lorenzale (1814-1889). Female Portrait (38 × 31).
Private collection.

reputation dating from 1846 when Count Raczinski, in a study of the plastic arts in Portugal, formed a not very flattering judgment of Portuguese painting in those days, contrasting it with the praise he lavished upon Milà and Lorenzale. On the other hand, we know the views expressed by the architect Elies Rogent in 1855 when visiting the churches and monuments of Munich, the capital of Ludwig I's Bavaria, in the company of Joaquim Espalter and Lorenzale, Rogent's brother-in-law. They admired without reservation Cornelius' murals representing the Nibelungen in the Royal Palace, but when they reached the Neue Pinakothek they thought it incongruous that the figures in the mural decoration should appear in Greek dress, seeing that it would not occur to the Germans to disguise themselves as ancient Greeks.

As for Espalter, his art was more elegant and realistic. Settled in Madrid, he carried out great mural compositions in public buildings.

The transition to Romanticism was already present in the work of some of Joan Carles Anglès' pupils, among whom numbered Arrau and his cousin Lluís Rigalt, already mentioned above in connection with his father, the painter of landscapes and theatre scenery Pau Rigalt.

Joaquim Espalter (1809-1880). Portrait of Mrs Espalter, 1852 (113 × 89).
Museum of Modern Art, Barcelona.

The Romantic attitude of these painters became very clear in the œuvre of many contemporaries, both landscapists and figure painters. This tendency was undoubtedly strengthened by the use of photography, a technique that was introduced into Barcelona in 1839 and spread very rapidly.

Consolidated by their stay in Italy and demonstrated so eloquently by Josep Galofre in his descriptions of landscapes quoted in an earlier chapter, the success of some of these painters now found external confirmation in the fact that two Catalan artists residing in Rome were designated by an international jury in 1845 to direct the official teaching of painting and sculpture

Ramon Martí Alsina (1826-1894). The Siesta (53 × 56).
Museum of Modern Art, Barcelona.

respectively in Mexico at the Academy of San Carlos. The painter chosen was Pelegrí Clavé, who had been in Rome as early as 1833. The years of his training as an artist were steeped in an international atmosphere; in a letter dated 1844, for example, Clavé refers to an international exhibition held in Rome he had competed in, and mentions several watercolours by the Swiss Corrodi and a *St Catherine* by the Tyrolean Charles Blaas.

While Milà and Lorenzale continued their task, other artists began to work by their side. One such artist was Ramon Martí i Alsina (Barcelona, 1826-1894). He had begun his studies in 1841, before Lorenzale joined the Llotja school as an instructor, and also taught there himself and was the only nineteenth-century Catalan painter to enjoy a large international reputation, in both America and Europe.

We might recall here, in rapid outline, the first stages of his training in Reus under the painter Domingo Soberano, and in Barcelona under Milà and Lorenzale, who supported him unreservedly and in 1857 obtained a scholarship from Barcelona's *Diputació* for him to travel to Rome, whereas Tomàs Padró and Antoni Caba won honourable mentions. The commission granted by the *Diputació* to travel to Morocco (1860) to paint various episodes of the African War brought him into contact with General Prim, who was also a native of Reus. The enormous canvas entitled *The Battle of Tetuán*, begun by Fortuny in Rome in 1861 after he had seen Horace Vernet's paintings at Versailles, is a work, albeit unfinished, of extraordinary expressive force. The landscape is natural and highly simplified, and the colour and movements of the figures are handled with great freedom, evincing nevertheless an excellent execution. One result of this and other journeys to Morocco was the permanent presence in his work of themes made fashionable by the painters known as *orientalists*. Fortuny was never to abandon them, combining such themes with an exceptional mastery of watercolour technique and a parallel predilection for painting figures kitted out with dress coats in the eighteenth-century fashion. Orientalism was also to take him to Andalusia, sojourning several times in Seville and most of all Granada. In Madrid he came into contact with the important painter Federico de Madrazo, who helped Fortuny to win access to official circles and encouraged his daughter Cecilia's marriage to the young painter. A later token of their engagement is the picture *The Spanish Wedding*, executed in two versions (1869-1870) which, thanks to the international dealer Alphonse Goupil, afforded him access to American collectors in Paris and the French critics.

Théophile Gautier, for example, devoted a rather kitch-ridden eulogy to him when comparing the painting to "a sketch by Goya retouched by Meissonier." Nevertheless, even earlier (1868), his success in Paris was so great that the dealer Théodore Duret wrote to Manet that an unsigned work of his would pass for a Fortuny, according to a notable letter mentioned by Francesc Fontbona. Promoter in Madrid and Barcelona of groups of watercolourists dedicated to his style, admired by fellow artists as well as French, Catalan, Málaga and North American collectors, highly esteemed in particular by the Swiss collector Walter Fol and the great French scholar Baron Charles Davillier, Marian Fortuny lost all this quite young, his life suddenly cut short at the height of his fame.

To some extent a prisoner of his own success and the requirements of dealers and collectors, during the last years of his brief existence Fortuny began to react against these limitations and this drove him to produce such works as *The Model* and *The Choice of the Model* (Corcoran Art Gallery, Washington), and *The Garden of the Poets*. In 1874, on a return visit to the Paris Salon, he criticized the event, showing his disappointment on seeing the paintings of artists whom he had admired some time before. Shortly afterwards he made a journey to London in the company of Baron Davillier, with whom he made the acquaintance of Vincent van Gogh, who represented the dealer Goupil in London at the time.

The Paris Universal Exhibition of 1878 dedicated a posthumous hall of honour to him containing 30 paintings, 13 of them belonging to the American collector Stewart. In the same year, the Catalan weekly *La llumanera de Nova York*, which was published in the United States at the time, devoted a special number to the artist with contributions by authors from Barcelona and Reus, and drawings by some American students and admirers, the best of whom were Robert Frederick Blum (1857-1903), William Merritt Chase (1849-1916), and Harry Humphrey Moore, who had been a personal friend of Fortuny's.

To return to Van Gogh, it is worth mentioning some allusions to Fortuny that appear in the Dutch painter's correspondence with both his brother Theo and Rappard. Commenting on Fortuny's watercolours, included among those of Italian artists, Van Gogh has this to say,

[1882]. ". . . These brilliant peacock feathers of the Italians that seem to multiply day by day . . . I would just as soon work as the buttons in a hotel as be a kind of watercolour manufacturer . . . I do not mean they are all like that . . . There are some cases whose work I appreciate—for example, Fortuny and Morelli, and at times Tapiró too . . . When I saw the

Marian Fortuny (1838-1874). The Rectory, 1870 (60 × 93).
Museum of Modern Art, Barcelona.

works for the first time—ten or twelve years ago—I was working for Goupil—I found them magnificent.

"What use are Boldini, Fortuny and even Regnault to us? What progress do we owe them?"

In January 1883, however, he varied his tone a little and rectified his remarks to some extent:

". . . In Goupil and Company's exhibition I have seen a large etching by Fortuny entitled *An Anchoress*, and two beautiful proofs of his, *Cabileño Dead* and *Vigil for the Dead*. I now greatly regret having written to you recently that I did not appreciate Fortuny's work. I found these pieces very beautiful . . . What happens is that the truth Fortuny has been able to express in these three etchings is lacking in a large number of his followers, who sacrifice everything to the technique that Fortuny has shown us in, for instance, *The Choice of the Model*."

With Fortuny's followers and imitators we come to what Eugeni d'Ors dubbed "the hours of the Sala Parés," that is to say, the world of international dealers, whose taste was dominated by the Paris Salons. Fontbona, on the other hand, preferred the term "art of the Restoration period" (of the Bourbons in Spain), although that did not occur until 1876 and the exhibition hall of the Sala Parés dates from the following year. Here we should first mention two of the great artist's personal friends, Josep Tapiró, who like Fortuny also hailed from Reus and has already been mentioned in the above quotation by Van Gogh, as well as Tomàs Moragas (Girona, 1837 - Barcelona, 1906); both were principally drawn to Moroccan themes. There were also many others, however, who devoted themselves to works with a European atmosphere, from eighteenth-century dress coats to an elegant and commercial interpretation of all kinds of themes. Within this wholly international genre encompassing artists of different backgrounds we shall single out such painters as Antoni Casanova i Estorach (Tortosa, 1847 - Paris, 1896), Francesc Miralles (Valencia, 1848 - Barcelona, 1901), Arcadi Mas i Fondevila (Barcelona, 1852 - Sitges, 1934), Romà Ribera (Barcelona, 1849-1935) and Francesc Masriera (Barcelona, 1842-1902).

Apart from Baldomer Galofre (Reus, 1846 - Barcelona, 1902) who, in his best Italian landscapes, preserved an echo of Fortuny's Neapolitan phase, the others, each in his own way, adhered to the official tendencies of the day.

The Sala Parés, an establishment founded in 1840 by the Parés family, though lacking a permanent exhibition hall until 1877, represented the culmination of the city's private galleries, with a series of forerunners that have been patiently enumerated by Feliu Elias when studying the circles in which Simó Gómez moved.

Casanova i Estorach and Francesc Galofre i Oller remained faithful to the genre of the great German history painting that would later inspire the inaptly named *socialist realism* of the mid-twentieth century. Such is the case, for example, with Casanova i Estorach's great compositions or Galofre i Oller's picture entitled *Bòria avall* (1892), conceived as an enormous diorama; the same trend also served as the model for the first large pictures exhibited by the youthful Pablo Ruiz Picasso, *First Communion* (1895), and to an even greater extent *Science and Charity* (1896).

When dealing with history and genre painting, I have already mentioned the figure of Josep Cusachs (Montpellier, 1851 - Barcelona, 1908), who abandoned the army to devote himself specifically to painting of military themes, in which he would display a distinguished and prolific activity, aided by the lessons of Edouard Detaille (Paris, 1848-1912), one of the most famous European painters in this field.

Francesc Miralles was born in Valencia in 1848, but from his childhood he lived in Barcelona where he was in contact with the well-to-do middle class and actually became part of their social sphere though the marriage of his sister Carmen to Dr Salvador Andreu. Until 1893 Miralles resided in Paris, where he had moved his parents and brothers; from there in the final years of

Josep Cusachs (1851-1908). The Battle of Arlaban, 1888 (75 × 115).
Museum of Modern Art, Barcelona.

Francesc Miralles (1848-1901). Spring in Paris, about 1895 (37 × 46).
Museum of Modern Art, Barcelona.

his life, he returned to Barcelona, where he died in 1901. Like many of his contemporaries, among whom the Belgian Alfred Stevens (Brussels, 1823 - Paris, 1906) stands out, he was greatly appreciated for his portraits and landscapes with figures, whose atmosphere is always rendered in a skilful yet facile manner.

Francesc Masriera (Barcelona, 1842-1902), member of a large dynasty of goldsmiths hailing from Mataró, was essentially a figure painter. In 1878 he exhibited *The Slave* in Paris, in the style favoured by Fortuny's orientalist followers, a tendency that he repeated in his *Odalisque*, exhibited in the French capital in 1889. The great genre compositions with a European or more specifically Barcelonan atmosphere provided him with work while limiting him with respect to the new forms of plastic expression that were being introduced before the end of the century. It is in this sense that an anonymous poet dedicated an epigram to him in 1901,

"If painting with great delicacy
jewels and silks and flowers
made the finest painters,
You would be one of them, Masriera."

Romà Ribera (1849-1935). Lady in an Evening Gown, 1893 (42 × 29).
Museum of Modern Art, Barcelona.

Francesc Masriera (1842-1902). The Winter of 1882 (80 × 61).
Museum of Modern Art, Barcelona.

Dionís Baixeras (1862-1943). Seascape, 1886 (90 × 150).
Museum of Modern Art, Barcelona.

The painting of Romà Ribera (Barcelona, 1849-1935) enjoyed a creative middle period in which the natural qualities of figures and compositions with contemporary themes display features in common with Francesc Masriera's work. Unfortunately, that period was followed by another in which one can say that the artist outlived himself to produce a series of completely conventional figures in seventeenth-century dress (musketeers, etc.).

Joan Ferrer i Miró (Vilanova i la Geltrú, 1850 - Barcelona, 1931) demonstrated qualities that won him a gold medal at the Barcelona Universal Exhibition of 1888 for the painting *Public Exhibition of a Picture*.

Now we must return to the days of Ramon Martí i Alsina and other—quite different—painters who began their training in his Barcelona studio.

The first, mentioned above when dealing with figure painters, was Joaquim Vayreda, founder of what is known as the Olot School. I should point out that as early as 1783 Olot boasted a school of drawing (still open today). Its first director was the Mataró painter Joan Carles Panyó, whose training was strictly neoclassicist. His successor—nominated for the sole merit of being Panyó's son-in-law—was Narcís Pascual, with very limited ambitions, who made his pupils copy engraved plates. One of them, with a basket of flowers and a snail crawling up it, is known from a drawing by Josep Berga i Boix, fellow pupil and friend of Joaquim Vayreda. The latter turned his eye to the painterly surroundings of the Olot countryside at the suggestion of Ramon Martí i Alsina, in whose studio he had been in Barcelona.

Although Vayreda always recognized Martí i Alsina's skill, in his inaugural speech at the Artistic Centre of Olot in 1870, he proclaimed his enthusiasm for the Romanticism of Chateaubriand and, in particular, identified himself with René, one of the protagonists of *Les Natchez*, illustrated with such Romantic sensibility by Gustave Doré.

Three or four trips to Paris starting in 1871 and his participation in the Salons of 1870, 1878, 1880 and 1881 with various works put him in touch with official French painting and the landscapes of the Barbizon School, whose head, Charles Daubigny, had apparently received a visit in 1866 from Marian Fortuny, who owned one of Daubigny's landscapes.

The quality and reality of the natural landscapes of Olot, already described in another chapter, were decisive in the painting of Joaquim Vayreda, just as they played a major role in the work of his brother Marian (Olot, 1853 - Barcelona, 1903)—a student of Gerôme's in Paris and Goupil's son-in-law, who had been Fortuny's dealer—his collaborator Melcior Domenge and Josep Berga i Boix (Olot, 1837-1914). The arrival of new followers, such as Enric Galwey, who transferred the lessons learnt to the landscapes of Garriga, along with the activity of hundreds of other painters consolidated the theme and assured success in rendering the surrounding countryside. Some of Galwey's memories have been included in the chapter on landscape.

The natural setting also influenced, somewhat episodically, two other excellent painters, namely, Dionís Baixeras (Barcelona, 1862-1943), in his landscapes and figures painted in Camprodon, just as in the portraits he executed of his wife in 1885, although the painter was better known for his beach scenes; and Modest Urgell (Barcelona, 1839-1919). With the latter painter, the influence was more diffuse and in the end would become a reciprocal process. Nevertheless, Baixeras and Urgell later adopted a painting with grey tones like that of Joaquim Vancells (Barcelona, 1865-1942), closely associated with Terrassa. Undoubtedly the most interesting personality for his art and his melancholic sensibility is that of Modest Urgell, painter, playwright and caricaturist, who had already exhibited in the Paris Salon of 1867 and influenced in his turn some of Joaquim Vayreda's works, as in the composition entitled *Sorrow*.

Santiago Rusiñol (1861-1931). Portrait of Miquel Utrillo (Paris), about 1891 (222 × 151).
Museum of Modern Art, Barcelona.

Santiago Rusiñol (1861-1931). Allegory of Painting, 1895 (140 × 190).
Cau Ferrat Museum, Sitges.

MODERNISM. PRECEDENTS, PARALLEL DEVELOPMENTS AND POSTERITY

At the turn of the century there occurred a partial rupture in the Catalan artistic world. It is quite logical that this break was partial and not total, given the norm in similar processes. Moreover, the protagonists had often been painting for years. When Eugeni d'Ors proposed giving a name to this moment he called it "The hours of Els Quatre Gats," taking it from the beerhall opened in 1897 in the Calle de Montsió in Barcelona and closed down in 1903. In fact, Els Quatre Gats (or The Four Cats) was the most famous and popular meeting place, but it was not the first. The story begins in the *Cau Ferrat*, the Barcelona studio of Santiago Rusiñol (Barcelona, 1861 - Aranjuez, 1931) and Enric Clarasó, inaugurated in 1885. The name came from Rusiñol's collection of ancient ironware transferred in 1893 to Sitges and placed in a new building, which was decorated one year later with great symbolist ceilings painted by Rusiñol with allegories of Poetry, Literature and Painting. Rusiñol had passed an early period of his career in that seaside town, the working and meeting place of a group of local luminist painters, such as Macari Oller, Joaquim de Miró (1849-1914), Joan Batlle (1855-1927), Càndid Duran and Antoni Almirall (1860-1905), as well as painters associated with the town (Joan Roig i Soler and Arcadi Mas i Fondevila).

Five *festes modernistes* or "modernist meetings" were celebrated on Rusiñol's initiative in Sitges between 1892 and 1899, convened under the standard of enthusiasm and poetic prose. In Reus, the *Modernist Almanac of Catalan Literature* (1891) ensured the diffusion of the term "modernist," both noun and adjective, the very existence of which certain overly critical scholars have recently rejected.

In the field of Catalan architecture the modernist period was dominated by Antoni Gaudí (Reus, 1852 - Barcelona, 1926), Lluís Domènech i Montaner (1850-1923) and Josep Puig i Cadafalch (Mataró, 1867 - Barcelona, 1957).

Ramon Casas (1866-1932). Plein air (Paris), 1890-1891 (51 × 66).
Museum of Modern Art, Barcelona.

The obvious forerunner of the beerhall Els Quatre Gats was the Chat Noir in Paris, a well-known café where Pere Romeu (Torredembarra, 1862 - Barcelona, 1909) had worked. Romeu settled temporarily in the United States at the same time as Miquel Utrillo (Barcelona, 1862 - Sitges, 1934); together they opened (bankrolled by a Chicago gentleman) an establishment around 1894, an adventure that proved unsuccessful. In 1895 Utrillo moved to Sitges, where he reached an agreement with the owner of the Café Continental, Pere Cuca, to transform it into the beerhall of Cau Ferrat. The business failed and it was then that Pere Romeu founded Els Quatre Gats in Barcelona. Memory of the famous beerhall remained so vivid in the mind of everyone who had been there that even in 1935, when Jaume Sabartés arrived in Paris to work as Picasso's secretary, Eugeni d'Ors defined him as an old *Quatre-Gatsman* and added, "Some day we must agree on trying to define the species, now close to extinction."

Before his stays in Paris, what we know of Rusiñol's pictorial production consists of traditional landscapes, not very different from those which many others were habitually turning out. In Barcelona, he studied under Tomàs Moragas, a friend and companion of Fortuny's, and owner of a large collection of antiques. Moragas also devoted himself to the Catalan landscape, together with the pictures of Moors and popular Italian characters. Since 1889 Rusiñol spent long periods in Paris, where he shared quarters with Miquel Utrillo, and showed many works at the Salons of 1888 and 1894, exhibiting together with the impressionists and symbolists in the latter Salon. From 1890 to 1930, he organized annual exhibitions in the Sala Parés with Ramon Casas (Barcelona, 1866-1932) and the sculptor Clarasó. Predominant in his painting and even more so in that of Ramon Casas were the greys which lend the art of the American James A. McNeill Whistler its individuality. Then he introduced the garden and landscape themes of Sitges, Majorca, Andalusia and Castile, and tended towards a decorative lyricism that fitted in with the poetic prose of his book *Prayers*, illustrated by Miquel Utrillo.

On the occasion of his stay in Majorca, the poet Joan Alcover described him as follows,

"Audacious, with pipe in your lips and pale cheeks,
You go wherever art finds shelter,
A little bitter your smile, your soul a little sick
With the fever of the ideal."

In Barcelona Ramon Casas had been the pupil of Joan Vicens (1830-1886), a correct portrait-ist, with a sure line, as well as a history painter. In 1883 he travelled to Paris to study with Carolus-Duran (1837-1917), the best-known portraitist in the French capital who enjoyed great fame in Madrid where he had participated in the National Exhibition of 1867. With a delicacy of nuances—whites, greys and pale greens—the works exhibited by Casas in the Paris Salons and the Sala Parés beginning in 1890 show a clear affinity with Rusiñol's art at a time when they both lived in the Moulin de la Galette in Montmartre. Casas' refined palette persists in works executed in Barcelona: *The Load*, between 1900 and 1903, *Afternoon Dance* and the two ceilings for the decoration of Els Quatre Gats: *The Tandem* (*Ramon Casas and Pere Romeu on a Tandem*, of 1897, and *Ramon Casas and Pere Romeu in an Automobile*, of 1901). The decoration of the Cercle del Liceu marked an inevitable affectation, within the framework of very sure drawing.

This quality also appeared in the posters that made Ramon Casas famous and in the hundreds of half-length and full-length portraits exhibited for the first time at the Sala Parés in 1899 and donated by the artist to Barcelona's Museum of Modern Art. It was precisely the impact of this exhibition that inspired Picasso to organize a similar exhibition in the hall of Els Quatre Gats. We might recall that Casas made an excellent drawing of Picasso in Montmartre which was published by Miquel Utrillo in the second of the reviews promoted by Ramon Casas, *Pel & Ploma*, or Fur and Feather. The first was called *Quatre Gats*.

The personality of Miquel Utrillo is that of an animator rather than a painter or draughts-man. Undoubtedly better educated than Rusiñol or Casas, he was not as gifted as the latter and lacked the stable financial position that the others had inherited. He spent some time in Paris in 1880 to study agronomy. In 1883 he met Suzanne Valadon; she bore him a son whom he recognized in 1891. Their son, Maurice Utrillo (1883-1956), would later make a name for himself in turn as a painter. In 1889 Miquel returned to Paris where he lived with Rusiñol and other friends. During the years 1893-1894 he lived in the United States; in his correspondence Utrillo recalls this time in his New York studio, decorated with reproductions of works by Velázquez, Forain, Willette, Toulouse-Lautrec, Puvis de Chavannes and Rodin. He exhibited paintings in Paris in 1895 and 1896. Although Utrillo divided his life between Sitges and Barcelona, he continued to travel abroad regularly. Years later he played a part in the construction and decoration of the Maricel Palace in Sitges and, together with Xavier Nogués, contributed to the project for the Pueblo Español (Spanish Village) on Montjuic, inaugurated in 1929.

Ramon Casas (1866-1932).
Ramon Casas and Pere Romeu
on a Tandem, 1897 (191 × 215).
Museum of Modern Art,
Barcelona.

Alexandre de Riquer (1856-1920). Poetry (stained glass window), about 1900 (142 × 60).
The Theatre Museum, Barcelona.

When they reached their artistic prime, Rusiñol and Casas could count on the support of the most prestigious Barcelona critic of the day, Raimon Casellas, who had published very significant commentary on Puvis de Chavannes, Whistler, Monet and the impressionist landscape, Burne-Jones and the Pre-Raphaelites, Eugène Carrière and Joan Francesc Raffaelli, when covering the exhibition held in Paris on the Champ-de-Mars in 1883.

Although the art of Rusiñol and Casas is not identical to that of their fellow *habitués* of Els Quatre Gats, it is convenient to set several figures of the earlier generation alongside them. The best of these was undoubtedly Josep Lluís Pellicer, the excellent draughtsman we have already mentioned. There were other draughtsmen, too, such as Apel·les Mestres (Barcelona, 1854-1936) and, above all, the prolific Alexandre de Riquer (Calaf, 1856 - Palma de Mallorca, 1920). Riquer was a great promotor of the Pre-Raphaelites in Catalonia, partly owing to his first visit to London in 1879, but mainly as a result of a long stay in England in 1893, after winning a gold medal in Chicago the same year. The ceilings of the monumental decoration of the Montserrat Monastery church, those published by Castellanos with allegories of Poetry and Music, and the series of eight ceilings in Barcelona's Museum of Modern Art, one of them dated 1887, are a very eloquent example of his art, as are hundreds of ex-libris, some stained glass windows (such as the one containing a representation of Poetry) and a vast repertory of posters.

His books of verse are full of allusions to his English friends. After the crowning period of modernism in 1910, he published a monograph on Robert Anning Bell. His relations with this milieu were the subject of a special study by Eliseu Trenc and Maria Àngela Cerdà.

His example, especially within the sphere of his ex-libris, had a notable influence on Josep Triadó (Barcelona, 1870-1929), Joaquim Renart (Barcelona, 1879-1961), Jaume Llongueras (Barcelona, 1883-1955) and Josep Maria Sert, of whom I shall make special mention further on. We should also recall that the diffusion of cultural trends within the world of these artists did not proceed in a single direction, such that in 1900 Riquer published an article that appeared in the first issue of the Barcelona review *Joventut* (Youth), a publication whose title was inspired by the German *Jugend*.

Adrià Gual (1872-1943). Dew, 1897 (72 × 130).
Museum of Modern Art, Barcelona.

Casellas had advocated a symbolist painting that boasted many other representatives. For example, Adrià Gual, draughtsman and playwright, one of the founders (in 1891) of the Wagnerian Association and author of an interesting painting-poem entitled *Dew*. The review *Luz* (Light) was one of the official organs of this symbolist tendency.

In his modernist phase, Eugeni d'Ors published similar works in another Barcelona review *Auba* (1904). Outstanding among the symbolists of the Cercle Artístic de Sant Lluc, in addition to Riquer, were Josep Maria Tamburini (Barcelona, 1856-1932), Joan Llimona (Barcelona, 1860-1926) and Joan Brull (Barcelona, 1863-1921), who went through an earlier phase of a realist nature (Rome, 1881 and Venice, 1883). Llimona, already mentioned above when dealing with religious painting, also cultivated other subjects, executing for instance great mural decorations such as those adorning the convent of Vic known as "of the Escorial," and especially the paintings for the dome of a chapel in Montserrat's Monastery of the Virgin. Brull peopled his woods and pools with damsels and nymphs, after painting historical topics and some of the first known landscapes of Tossa on the Costa Brava.

Joan Brull (1863-1921). Reverie, about 1898 (200 × 141).
Museum of Modern Art, Barcelona.

Josep Maria Sert (Barcelona, 1874-1945), who displayed a markedly baroque temperament, came from the same milieu, having studied under Pere Borell. He made a name for himself in 1900 during the great Universal Exhibition in Paris when the decorator Bing commissioned him to execute paintings for the dining-room of the pavilion called *Art Nouveau, Homage to Pomona*, a title that gave French and English art the equivalent of *modernism* in Catalonia.

Combining precedents which run from Tintoretto and Rubens to Tiepolo, Goya and Piranesi, Sert was for many years the fashionable international decorator for profane and religious themes. I have already mentioned the commission for the decoration of Vic Cathedral, which Sert obtained thanks to his friend, and religious adviser to the Cercle Artístic de Sant Lluc, Dr Josep Torras i Bages. An initial exhibition, in full colour, was held in Paris in 1904 and although he was criticized for the profane and spectacular mood of the experiment, his success with the public and clients proved extraordinary. The list of commissions and projects is exceptional: Vic, Barcelona, Paris, Brussels, San Sebastián, London, New York, Palm Beach,

Geneva, Buenos Aires, Sitges, Palamós and Palma de Mallorca preserve—or once owned—examples of Sert's paintings, executed over a long period between the years 1900 and 1945. The decoration of the Salon of the Chronicles in Barcelona's town hall (1928-1929), with paintings alluding to the Catalans' expedition to the East, is a very characteristic example. He conceived of painting as a total art that advanced towards the future, so much so that in 1942 he wrote,

"The architect has confined himself to piling up materials in a certain order . . . in exactly the same way that the shell adapts itself to the needs of the animal that lives inside it. So that the shell can support itself, man has always adhered to the straight line.

"This unchangeable law does not exist today and man has freed himself from the fatality of the straight line . . . Before us opens up a future that will allow us to curve the walls of a building, in just the same way as our forebears, who experimented with twisting columns."

Nevertheless, architecture and painting did not normally develop along the lines he had imagined.

The process of working out Sert's great compositions began with photographic studies, sometimes with great masses of subsidiary figures, studies executed with the collaboration of Leonard Mancosi. Another assistant, De la Chategneray, prepared the great bases of silvered or gilt canvases, covered — in collaboration with Miquel Massot (Barcelona, 1883 - Paris, 1968) — with uniform coats of paint retouched and finished off by Sert.

Aleix Clapés (1850-1920). Portrait of Manuel Dalmau Oliveres (120 × 90).
Museum of Modern Art, Barcelona.

Simó Gómez (1845-1880).
Portrait of the Fine-Furniture Craftsman Francesc Vidal,
1875 (73 × 52). Museum of Modern Art, Barcelona.

Francesc Gimeno (1858-1927).
The Faithful Companion (Infant with a Dog), 1897 (76 × 57).
Sala Collection, Montserrat Monastery Museum.

Aleix Clapés (Vilassar de Dalt, 1850 - Barcelona, 1920), an imaginative decorator who collaborated with Antoni Gaudí, was an interesting, though uneven, artist. His compositions and portraits with blurred outlines recall only partially the art of Eugène Carrière, a very famous painter in his day. An immediate follower of Carrière's was the Catalan painter Lluïsa Vidal (Barcelona, 1876-1918), sister of Frederic Vidal, who designed a number of modernist *cloisonné* stained glass windows; both were children of the fine-furniture craftsman Francesc Vidal (1848-1914).

The Majorcan Gaspar Homar (Brunyola, 1870 - Barcelona, 1953), the best of the modernist decorators in Barcelona, had also worked in the studio of Francesc Vidal (whose portrait was painted by Simó Gómez in 1875). Assisted by the draughtsman Josep Pey (Barcelona, 1875-1956), he executed marquetry mosaics and ceilings that display an exceptionally refined art. Another member of his atelier was the painter and ceramicist Antoni Serra, whom we have mentioned above when dealing with painting of social themes. We also know of Serra's association with another symbolist painter, Sebastià Junyent (Barcelona, 1865-1908).

Within the bounds of these particular themes, we should also mention an artist preoccupied with social themes and the effects of artificial light, Lluís Graner (Barcelona, 1863-1929), who painted the portrait of a critic who was emblematic of modernism and symbolism, Raimon Casellas (1894). In 1904 Graner set up the organization of audio-visual spectacles. Later he went to the United States, although he eventually returned to Barcelona where he remained until his death.

Francesc Gimeno (Tortosa, 1858 - Barcelona, 1927) forms a special case, achieving a quite expressive realism in his figures, as in the splendid portrait of his daughter with a dog (*The*

Lluís Graner (1863-1929). Portrait of the Author and Art Critic Raimon Casellas, 1894 (185 × 90).
Museum of Modern Art, Barcelona.

Faithful Companion), dated 1891 (Sala Collection, Montserrat Monastery Museum). His numerous landscapes are correct although less personal.

Fontbona, after having tried to dismiss the existence of modernism, suggested the term post-modernists for a series of very different artists, perhaps in the same way that the name post-impressionists applies to some painters immediately after impressionism.

Yet whatever the label, we can include in this phase the early period of Joaquim Torres Garcia, and, above all, Nicolau Raurich (Barcelona, 1871-1945), Isidre Nonell (Barcelona, 1873-1911) Joaquim Mir (Barcelona, 1873-1940), Hermen Anglada Camarasa (Barcelona, 1871 - Pollença, 1959) and Marian Pidelaserra (Barcelona, 1877-1946), figure among the most interesting practitioners along with several periods of Picasso's extremely rich and multifaceted production.

Isidre Nonell is undoubtedly the most painterly of the Catalan artists in the first decade of the twentieth century. Like so many others, he had begun to paint in an impersonal style at the end of the nineteenth century and was one of the members of the *Colla de Sant Martí* (Company of St Martin), in whose works the landscape of city outskirts predominates. Following his stay in the valley of Boí and the Val d'Aran in 1896 with Ricard Canals and Juli Vallmitjana, Nonell's creative drawing underwent an important change which would later make its way into his painting.

Although the phrase often attributed to Nonell "I paint and that's it!" or "I paint, and off with you!" has since become proverbial, it probably reflects no more than the desire to be left undisturbed. His correspondence with Casellas, made known thanks to the efforts of Lluís-Emili Bou, is very interesting. Nonell, accompanied by Ricard Canals, arrived in Paris in 1897. On 3 March Nonell writes that he appreciates the impressionists less than Puvis de Chavannes, Whistler, Sargent and Carrière. He praises the drawings of Forain, Ibels and Steinlen. On 30 March he already admits his enthusiasm for Monet and Degas, and for a Renoir in the Durand-Ruel gallery. After the success of the first exhibition of his drawings in Paris (5 January-6 February 1898), in another letter dated 26 February he now applauds the works of Degas, Monet and Manet, among which figure the pictures from the Camondo collection and Monet's cathedrals. He also lingers over Daumier's engravings and adds, "Of the draughtsmen, one of those who interested me most was Lautrec." The first exhibition of Nonell's drawings in Els Quatre Gats took place in December 1898; the themes represented and the quality of these early works are already those of the years to come. In 1899 Nonell returned to Paris and gave an exhibition there in Ambroise Vollard's gallery, his work still peopled with the outcasts of society, idiots and gypsies. Later he returned to Barcelona, although between 1902 and 1910 he would unfailingly take part in the collective Parisian exhibitions of the *Indépendants*. Even if he painted the occasional portrait in a far from conventional manner, gypsy women made up his habitual subject until 1907. It should be born in mind that this fact has an obvious parallel in the literature of Juli Vallmitjana, whose characters are usually Catalan gypsies speaking a very distinctive tongue. From 1907 to 1910 his portraits of female figures alternate between gypsy women and women who are apparently white. Lastly, he painted a remarkable cycle of still lifes in 1910. Nevertheless, unlike all the other Catalan painters of his day (including Ricard Canals), Nonell was not seeking an almost touristic picturesque in gypsy women, but rather a combination of personal touch and a kind of abstraction. During the first phase, seagreens and blues predominate, like those used by Picasso in his Blue Period and even later, when he executed such exceptional works as the composition *Life*. In the last period of Nonell's production earthcolours and ochre and pink tones, alternating with bluish, grey and skyblue tones, are common. This no doubt reflects the artist's predilection for the material and colours, outside any purely anecdotal element.

Even though Nonell's qualities distinguish him from many other painters and draughtsmen of his day, there were some who showed clear affinities with him, such as the group *Els Negres*, among whom figure Manuel Ainaud (Barcelona, 1885-1932) and Claudi Grau, who closed the exhibition hall of Els Quatre Gats in 1903. I should also mention the draughtsman Ricard Opisso (Tarragona, 1880 - Barcelona, 1966), the painter Joaquim Biosca (Barcelona, 1882-1932) and,

Isidre Nonell (1873-1911). Figure, 1908 (65 × 54).
Museum of Modern Art, Barcelona.

Joaquim Mir (1873-1940). Cala de Sant Vicenc, Majorca, about 1905 (280 × 400).
Sala Collection, Montserrat Monastery Museum.

a little earlier, Carles Casagemas (Barcelona, 1880 - Paris, 1901), a close friend of Picasso's who died tragically.

The case of Joaquim Mir stands quite apart. In the early years of his career, he cultivated a naturalistic luminism similar to that practised by other Catalan and foreign painters. One of his landscapes representing cabbage fields seems to have been executed under the influence of the Dutch painter Evert Pieters (Amsterdam, 1856 - Laren, 1932). A picture by Pieters with the same subject was awarded a prize in Barcelona in 1898. The change to a decorative and symbolic, though somewhat excessive, use of colour came about on the occasion of his journey to Majorca in 1901, where he stayed at the same time as the Belgian painter Degouwe de Nunques, who had ties with Rusiñol and Mir. This Majorcan period was one of the most notable for the painter and was prolonged in Barcelona by some large stained glass windows and the decoration of the Trinxet House, commissioned by one of the artist's maternal uncles. Next came another very noteworthy stage in his career, that is, the time he spent in Reus and painted in the Tarragona countryside. He tended to express himself by isolated patches of very intense colours that seem infused with an exceptional poetic feeling. Later, in the Vallès, the Garraf, on the banks of the Ebro and in the Pyrenees, Mir's essentially landscape art began to merge with the traditional formulas.

Nicolau Raurich often worked with very thick impasto, contrasting hot, violent tones and luminous bright blue shadows.

The crowning moments of decorative and colouristic sentiment also appeared as an important element in Hermen Anglada Camarasa's painting. After a more or less academic phase, he began, in Paris around 1900, an exceptionally lyrical and decorative period, in which whites and yellows predominate, forging an art reminiscent of Picasso's creative work in those years. Anglada enjoyed a long period of great international success, executing compositions with various typical figures in which he cultivated the local colour of such Spanish regions as Aragon, Andalusia and Valencia.

This formula ensured that his work widely diffused throughout Europe and America. Before exhausting this wave of success, Camarasa was wise enough to retire to Majorca, where he continued a conventional, yet estimable, kind of painting in which landscapes, flowers and figures predominated, including themes of underwater fauna, much more realistic than one might imagine. We find a synthesis of all these elements in the large composition of a mermaid among fish in Palma de Mallorca's Gran Hotel (the creation of the architect Lluís Domènech i Montaner), next to one of Joaquim Mir's largest landscapes and another by Santiago Rusiñol, full of almond trees in blossom.

The same lyrical Majorca inspired many other painters who took up residence on the island, such as Sebastià Junyer Vidal (Castelló d'Empúries, 1878 - Barcelona, 1966), a friend of Picasso's in their adolescence. Later, in the 30s, Joan Junyer (Barcelona, 1904), son of Carles and brother of Sebastià, also elected to work there, producing compositions with typically Majorcan subjects; even more recently Josep Coll Bardolet (Campdevànol, 1912), born in the Ripoll region, has lived in Majorca since 1940.

Marian Pidelaserra, who only treated Majorcan themes occasionally, is quite another case. His desire to maintain absolute creative freedom forced him to spend periods of pictorial inactivity in order to achieve financial independence by other means.

Nicolau Raurich (1871-1945). Latin Sea, about 1910 (119 × 149).
Museum of Modern Art, Barcelona.

His group was called *El Rovell de l'Ou* (The Yolk), a meeting place where they edited the manuscript review *Il Tiberio*. The artistic personality of each member of the group displays complete independence, their only link being the bonds of friendship that drew them together.

As was usual at the end of the nineteenth century, Pidelaserra's earliest works conformed to the luminist naturalism than can be observed in some of his landscapes of the Cerdagne (birthplace of his master, Pere Borrell). In 1899-1901 we find Pidelaserra in Paris, together with Pere Ysern i Alié, practising a sensitive painting which derives in part from Monet's cathedrals. Nevertheless, some landscapes (*The Green Baths, The Yellow Baths*) already display a different taste. Ysern stayed within the bounds of a commercial and already traditional continuation of impressionism, whereas Pidelaserra developed towards a very personal form of pointillism with works of such quality as the series of Montseny landscapes, exhibited in the Barcelona Athenaeum, that earned him his first critical notice in print, a lyrical and poetic appreciation by Francesc Pujols. A little earlier in Barcelona (1902), he had executed a collective portrait of the Déu family, which created a great stir. In 1905 he took part in a collective exhibition with Ysern, Nogués, Sebastià Junyer and Emili Fontbona (sculptor) in the Sala Parés, which proved a financial disaster. From 1929 to 1934 he painted landscapes of the Vallès, still lifes and portraits. In the closing period of his career he painted many landscapes (Val d'Aran, 1941-1944; the Aragonese Pyrenees, 1942; Majorca, 1945), alternating them with the two great series of compositions on the life of Jesus (1939-1942; 24 canvases) and *The Conquered* (1943-1945; 24 canvases). These compositions with figures, revealing a great mastery of colour, sparked violent criticism because they clearly showed the painter's rejection of painting from live models, in spite of Xavier Nogués' advice to the contrary. This was very similar to the reaction inspired by the last period of Josep Aragay's painting. Pidelaserra is a painter with many contrasts and notable successes, always interesting, although not always to everyone's taste. In the postwar years he found a circle of students and friends among several young artists (Oriol Jansana, Ignasi Mundó).

We can include other independent artists in the final period between modernism and post-modernism, for instance the prolific Ramon Pichot (Barcelona, 1871 - Paris, 1925), who

Joan Junyer (1904). Bucolic (90 × 117).
Museum of Modern Art, Barcelona.

Sebastià Junyer (1878-1966). The Angelus at Vespers (Majorca), 1922 (52 × 138).
Museum of Modern Art, Barcelona.

divided his life between Cadaqués, the Calle de Montcada, Barcelona and Parisian circles; and Xavier Gosé (Alcalá de Henares, 1876 - Lleida, 1915), illustrator of the Parisian review *Assiette au Beurre*, for which he drew elegant ladies and sporting subjects.

Both of these artists painted and drew compositions with figures, while working as illustrators, as did all of those who collaborated on the satirical Barcelonan review *Papitu*. Claudi Castelucho (Barcelona, 1870 - Paris, 1927) also cultivated themes taken from Spanish folklore and set up in Montparnasse a shop selling painters' materials that was frequented by many artists.

Ignasi Mundó (1918). Café Interior (34 × 49).
Private collection.

Ricard Canals (1876-1931). Portrait of Mrs Amouroux de Canals, about 1903 (101 × 68).
Museum of Modern Art, Barcelona.

By way of a colophon to this chapter, I should also make a reference to the first stages marking the art of Joaquim Sunyer (Sitges, 1874-1956) and Ricard Canals (Barcelona, 1876-1931). Sunyer was already in Paris before Canals' and Novell's arrival there. In 1889 the Sunyer family moved to Barcelona where Sunyer himself entered the School of Fine Arts in 1890. He was still studying there in 1894, with Mir, Nonell, Torres Garcia and Canals, but very soon they began to paint as independents. In Barcelona Sunyer was already familiar with the Parisian illustrated reviews, through which he was to make his first contact with Steinlen's art. Like many others, he went through a luminist phase (*Cabbage Field at Sitges*), but in 1896 his drawings published in *La Vanguardia* clearly showed resonances of Steinlen. Later these were consolidated in Paris by an interesting series of graphic works, in which his illustrations for *The Soliloquies of the Poor Man* by Jean Rictus (1897) are outstanding. Sunyer's copious Paris production up to 1905 followed the tendency of the Nabis, but was abruptly interrupted by a journey to Madrid and Avila in 1905-1906.

Canals' first works are often confused with those of Nonell in Paris, although his gypsies tend to be portrayed with an exaggerated "Spanishness," perhaps on the orders of his dealer Durand-Ruel, who sent the artist to Seville in 1900 to seek themes with *character*. This also explains the organization of an exhibition of Canals' works in the French dealer's New York gallery and his repeted trips to Madrid, Galicia and Andalusia. Canals came into direct contact with works by old Spanish artists (Velázquez, Goya) and bought paintings by them for his dealer. At the same time, Sunyer spent long evenings in Paris in the company of Renoir, who was already an old man. Renoir's influence on Canals is obvious in the portraits executed around 1907, before and after Canals abandoned Paris to settle in Barcelona. Examples are the portraits of Rosa Amouroux, wife of Antoni Canals, the painter's elder brother. In this final Parisian period, Canals deepened his friendship with Picasso. Thus, when Canals painted a great composition in which their respective companions, Benedetta Bianco and Fernande Olivier, are shown watching a bullfight—and wearing Spanish mantillas for the event—Picasso took advantage of the occasion to paint the portrait of Señora Canals; the painting now hangs in the Picasso Museum in Barcelona. Canal's great canvas is also on display in Barcelona.

Arístides Maillol (1861-1944). Woman with a Parasol, about 1890 (193 × 149).
Musée d'Orsay, Paris.

NOUCENTISM

Between modernism and the artistic periods that follow, there is much greater continuity than there exists between the same periods and what we now call *noucentism*. I must caution the reader, however, that the term is ambiguous, for Eugeni d'Ors christened a series of quite heterogeneous artists as noucentists, from a few decadents *à la* Aubrey Beardsley, such as Ismael Smith, Marian Andreu and Laura Albéniz, to those artists who were cultivating a Mediterranean classicism at the time.

At all events, there did exist clear indications of a certain classicizing sentiment which had begun with painters like Puvis de Chavannes, the object of a special homage at the Fifth Exhibition of Art in Barcelona in 1907. It is not irrelevant that the review succeeding *Pel & Ploma* and *Joventut* were called *Forma* (1904-1907) and *Empori* (1907). The last-named title was taken from the Greek colony of Empúries, which began to be excavated scientifically in 1907, one of the starting points for what has been called the *myth of Greek Catalonia*.

In this trend, however, as in so many others, Picasso showed himself a pioneer, if we bear in mind the Mediterranean landscapes with lateen-sailed ships and female nudes that predominate in drawings made between 1902 and 1903.

This classicism can also be observed in some of Picasso's compositions painted in Gósol in 1906 which display a range of pinks, greys and sky-blues. The sea is absent from these works as a direct model owing to the geographical setting, yet we should not forget that at this moment the noucentist sculptor Enric Casanova was also in Gósol with Picasso and that both were reading the book *Enllà (Beyond)* by the poet Joan Maragall, which had just come off the press. In Gósol's *Carnet Català (Catalan Notebook)*, next to the French translation of the poem *Vistes al Mar* (Views of the Sea), which begins, *"One by one, like virgins to the dance, the ships slip away on the sea..."* Picasso drew three female nudes as the Three Graces.

In the Roussillon, the most representative artist—who enjoyed international fame—of this "return to the Mediterranean" was undoubtedly Arístides Maillol (Banyuls, 1861-1944). Before reaching the highpoint of his creative work as a sculptor, Maillol went through an interesting period when he was in contact with Gauguin and the pointillists, a contact that is apparently due to the presence in the Roussillon of the collector Henri de Monfreid, one of Gauguin's personal friends. In Paris Maillol joined forces with the Nabis. On the other hand, Maillol's most significant Catalan friendships go back to earlier times. They include the Roussillon poet and watercolour landscapist Josep Sebastià Pons (Illa, 1886-1962), the sculptor and painter Manolo Hugué and the painters Joaquim Sunyer and Josep de Togores.

An identical programme of Mediterraneanism can be found in the editorial of the first issue of the review *Empori*, published in 1907,

". . . To bring to life, to make real, every day, every hour, the generous universal collaboration of the thinkers, the inventors, the historians, the artists, the poets; to bring from one place to the other, from certain men to other men, from certain coteries to other coteries, the prolongation, the continuation of the conversation that flourished during the glorious dawn of our civilization under the porticos of Athens, on the dusty Pyrenean road, in the cool shades of the gardens of Academe. . ."

This neoclassical programme also inspired the painter Joan Llaverias (he actually changed his surname to Llaveriotes) to execute a series of landscapes in watercolour of the Costa Brava, under the generic title of *Greek Catalonia* (1906).

Undoubtedly there was an inevitable artificiality about the programme, but the ideological pressure of this milieu was very strong and it was that pressure that impelled Enric Prat de la Riba, president of the *Diputació* of Barcelona (and later of the *Mancomunitat*), urged in turn by Eugeni d'Ors, to commission Joaquim Torres Garcia to decorate the Hall of St George in the Palace of the *Generalitat* in Barcelona. That artist, a student in Barcelona in 1893, had made a name for himself as a draughtsman and poster-designer at the height of the modernist period

Joaquim Torres Garcia (1875-1949).
Minerva Presenting the Muse of Philosophy to the Other Nine Muses (detail), 1911 (in full 124 × 385).
Institute of Catalan Studies, Barcelona.

and a few years later made his first attempt at mural decoration in one of the halls of Barcelona's town hall (1910). Nevertheless, the attempt was not a success and Eugeni d'Ors, who had been the patron of the experiment, wanted to compensate for the failure with a new, much more ambitious commission. Torres Garcia, born in Montevideo of a Catalan father, was sent to Italy to draw inspiration from the technique of mural painting. The doubtless well-meant test owed much to Puvis de Chavannes (as he himself confessed later). In 1912 he finished the central ceiling, called *Eternal Catalonia*. It was followed by another four until, with the death of Prat de la Riba, Josep Puig i Cadafalch—the architect and Riba's successor—suspended the continuation of the fifth, *Industry*. Various factors doubtless played a part in this decision and perhaps the most important of all was the radical change in the work's conception with the introduction of workers, men in top hats, an aeroplane and a locomotive. As for the fourth ceiling executed, which bore the motto *The storm is no more than a symbol*, Eugeni d'Ors' statement that this phrase was an obstacle to the work's continuation is untrue; it was in fact a line from Goethe's *Faust* that Josep Torras i Bages quoted with great praise in 1894 in a lecture given to the Cercle Artístic de Sant Lluc, at which the above-mentioned critic must have been present.

In keeping with the atmosphere in which he lived, Torres Garcia's four children were called August, Olímpia, Ifigènia and Horaci. The artist set up a school of decoration in Sarrià which Josep Obiols and Enric Casanovas attended, among others.

Later, Torres Garcia moved to Terrassa, settling in Mon Repòs, in a neoclassical house which he decorated personally, and executed other murals before travelling to Paris, Italy and America, always keeping in touch with his Barcelona friends, though already in the avant-garde art world.

During his stay in Catalonia, from 1913 onwards, he published *Notes on Art* and other writings of a theoretical nature. Between 1914 and 1915, the review of the School of Decoration was illustrated with works by Josep Obiols, Teresa Lostau (Xavier Nogués' first wife) and Josep Maria Marquès Puig, son of a painter who was a contemporary of Alexandre de Riquer; all of these artists, moreover, produced very interesting works.

Here is a sample of Torres Garcia's theoretical writings from 1913,

"To us, more fitted for the cultivation of art than the artists of the Northern nations, it falls by right to revive the great culture of Greece and Rome in all its youth in quite modern works, original like everything that is genuinely alive. . .

"In neighbouring France, a southerner like ourselves, the great Puvis de Chavannes, did exactly what we ought to be doing. He grafted the genius of his race on to the Graeco-Latin

Francesc Galí (1880-1965). Scenes from *Don Quixote* relating to the character's stay in Barcelona, 1959. Decorations for one of the rooms of Barcelona's town hall.

culture. Nevertheeless, being less southern than we are, his admirable art turns out to be less warm, less pure, too, less topical, in a word, less *classical.''*

The neoclassicism of the *peplos*, advocated so uncompromisingly by the ex-modernists Eugeni d'Ors and Torres Garcia, attracted poets like Josep Carner, author in 1906 of some sophisticated *Delicious Fruits*, often considered as one of the starting points of the noucentist aesthetic. For all that, Torres Garcia's change of theme in his ceiling *Industry* showed that he too was beginning to be tired of the movement. As early as 1906, Josep Pijoan, for his part, found the artificiality of *Delicious Fruits* and the way in which Eugeni d'Ors contrasted them with Maragall's *Enllà* unbearable. Pijoan, as Glòria Casals quite rightly remembers, declared, ''Oh, the ancient world, the ancient world! How different it is from what its inexperienced proselytes imagine!'' This reminds me of Elies Rogent's sensible criticism when faced with the pseudo-Greek tunics of the paintings in Munich's Neue Pinakothek.

From Torres Garcia's neoclassicism rises a branch, neither the only nor the oldest, of what we now know by the name of noucentism, which, at all events, brings us close to the plastic formulation of the *Almanach dels noucentistes*, published in 1911.

It must be borne in mind, as I have already stated more than once when dealing with artistic trends, that noucentism is not homogeneous, although the movement does possess specific common denominators.

The principal line of descent, in my opinion, is that indicated by the direct followers of Francesc d'A. Galí, in whose immediate circle were found other artists, Xavier Nogués, Joaquim Sunyer and Manolo Hugué, for instance.

Galí, in addition to his posters and mural paintings, enjoyed a great reputation as a teacher, with a drive and an ability that have been frequently praised. Galí gave up his architectural studies around 1897 and eventually studied under the painter Claudi Hoyos, in a milieu close to the Cercle Artístic de Sant Lluc. Around 1902 he founded a school of art that later adopted the name Academy.

One of his pupils, Josep Aragay, painter and ceramicist, wrote the following in 1915,

''. . . Galí awakes the aptitudes of each of us; he is not sought out as a teacher by those who want to go about disguised like players in a farce, whether it be a *noucentista* or a student who harks back to the previous century. He will not tell anyone what colour to paint trees, as in other times, nor will he teach him what the fashion of the day is. Let those hasten to go there who, still being young and in need of advice, do not hope for anything from anybody outside themselves, because in Galí they will find not the man who teaches what he knows, but the man who teaches them to know.''

In 1917 the critic and ceramicist Josep Llorens i Artigas affirmed that ''Galí's work in his Academy was more than that of a teacher of drawing, it was that of an educator; he understood that artists are not made; at the most they are awakened, and consequently he was not preoccupied with creating people who knew how to draw a nose or a foot correctly, but with creating people capable of feeling art.''

Conversations, excursions, attendance at concerts, all formed part of the Academy's training, continued later in the Advanced School of Fine Crafts and the Summer School of the *Mancomunitat.*

The Academy produced artists who had much in common with Galí, Josep Aragay and Manuel Humbert for instance, as well as painters of a very different stamp, Rafael Benet, Ignasi Mallol, Francesc Vayreda and Enric Cristòfol Ricart, Jaume Mercadé and Joan Miró, about whom I shall speak in more detail when dealing with the avant-gardes.

I must complete the first of the groups with Josep de Togores, although his early career was quite different.

Among the artists whom we could consider as belonging to *the old generation* figures Pere Torné Esquius (Sant Martí de Provençals, 1875 - Flavancourt, 1936), who devoted himself to an intimist painting praised by Maragall that is not too far from several of the Nabis. Also worth mentioning is Ricard Canals, whom we have referred to above with respect to the stages of his art akin to the early Nonell and under the influence of Renoir, around 1907. On his return to

Barcelona, Lluís Plandiura's protection induced him to lead the group called *Les Arts i els Artistes* (The Arts and the Artists). The influence of his visits to the Prado Museum produced a certain academicism in his art which was combined with a change of palette to greens and blues that seems to derive from Cézanne.

By way of contrast, there is Joaquim Sunyer's case, in which the lesson of Cézanne turned the painter towards an obvious structuralism, combined with a palette of cold tones, his sole point of contact with Canals. After an uncertain transitional period, his art settled down around 1910, flourishing in landscapes and compositions with figures executed during the painter's stays

Joaquim Sunyer (1874-1956). Pastoral, 1910-1911 (106 × 152).
Joan Maragall Estate, Barcelona.

in Sitges, which he alternated with sojourns in Ceret and Majorca. During this period, concentrated on the years 1910-1917, although prolonged far beyond, Sunyer's style was consolidated and stabilized, even though this meant foregoing public prestige. Miquel Utrillo's insistence earned him quite favourable commentary from Joan Maragall in 1910, when he made a special eulogy of *Pastoral*, a Mediterranean landscape with a female nude, acquired years later by the poet's children.

Sunyer maintained strong ties with the sculptor Manolo Hugué (Barcelona, 1872 - Caldes de Montbui, 1945), with whom he lived in Ceret. Manolo's very interesting and personal painting offers a much more vivid chromatic range than Sunyer's, using touches of red, emerald green and yellow set in marked contrast on grey grounds, works that only share with Sunyer's their

Manolo Hugué (1872-1945). Portrait of Totote, about 1931 (61 × 50).
Manolo Hugué Museum, Diputació de Barcelona, Caldes de Montbui.

preoccupation with structure. His earliest compositions belong to the modernist period; Manolo's most personal, however, were created later, in the 30s.

Xavier Nogués was undoubtedly one of the most esteemed and representative noucentist artists. If his earlier career began in Barcelona, in Pere Borell's Academy and the group *El Rovell de l'Ou (The Yolk)*, his personal orientation remained very different. He spent a period in Paris in the Colarossi Academy, in the Grande Chaumière, and returned to Catalonia in 1904. Later he made a number of other trips—albeit always brief ones—to the French capital and between 1927 and 1929 travelled throughout Spain on the occasion of the preparatory studies for the Spanish Village of Montjuic. Nevertheless, his activity and iconography were always centred on Catalan figures and landscapes, of which he was the most representative interpreter.

Drawings and caricatures, engravings, easel paintings, mural decorations, ceramics (with the help of Teresa Lostau) and enamelled stained glass (with the technical collaboration of Ricard Crespo) make up his prolific œuvre which displays a refined style in the forms and tones while using popular themes. He had already forged a personal style by 1909 which, after 1914, appears thoroughly perfected. A short time later, around 1915, he executed a great group of mural paintings, in which blue predominates, for the *bodega* of the Galerías Layetanas. Lluís Plandiura commissioned him to decorate a hall in his house in the Calle de Ribera in Barcelona, where he collaborated with Francesc Galí and other artists sharing a style renewed by the world of Art Deco. The work was completed in 1927 and shortly afterwards he undertook the decoration of the office of the mayor of Barcelona. His great series of drawings, such as that entitled

Xavier Nogués (1873-1941). Sunday Afternoon, 1923 (60 × 75).
Museum of Modern Art, Barcelona.

Manuel Humbert (1890-1975). Self-Portrait, about 1920 (31 × 19.5).
Private collection.

Manuel Humbert (Barcelona, 1890-1975), former student of the Galí Academy, later worked in Paris, where he struck up a close friendship with Amedeo Modigliani. That was the period when he executed a number of canvases and gouaches with small highly stylized figures. Later, in Barcelona, Humbert began to make use of short brushstrokes like those in some of Galí's canvases. A collective portrait of the old Taixonera collection displays a realism reminiscent of pop art. He also produced ceramics.

Although coming from Torres Garcia's milieu, Josep Obiols (Sarrià, 1894 - Barcelona, 1967) had far more in common with Galí; indeed, he is the most representative and balanced of the noucentist painters and the only one to preserve a stable tendency for nearly three quarters of a century. In the period of the *Mancomunitat* he designed the poster for the Protective Association of Catalan Teaching and illustrated many of the association's books; moreover, it was Obiols who created prototypes and female models exemplifying early noucentism. He travelled to Italy in 1920 with the poet Carles Riba. Carles-Jordi Guardiola, commenting on the correspondence arising from the journey, again falls into the trap of considering Eugeni d'Ors to be the *inventor* of noucentism and the movement's particular view of Italy, oblivious of the testimony of Torres Garcia and some very significant verses by Joan Maragall to the sculptor Josep Clarà (1910), in which he speaks of the artist's sculptures:

"They are sisters of those immortal daughters
of our sea at the other shore;
but did not hear the signs of that age
and so they missed their sweet chance.
And now, at the call of our evoking artist
they have risen to the light and they are found
with the same serenity of the antique genius,
but with a new tenderness."

As always, we are faced with the obsession with a first Renaissance, frustrated in Catalonia by historical circumstances, which the *Mancomunitat*, from its inception, sought to retrieve.

Lluís Guarro's music room in Sarrià (1923) was one of the first milestones marking an itinerary that persisted in spite of the First Dictatorship and, following the fall of that regime, continued to exist in the ceilings of the Chamber of Commerce (1938) and the design of the *Generalitat*'s bank notes during the Civil War. After his exile, he resumed his activities in the 40s in the sacristy and other parts of Montserrat Monastery, until he undertook the decoration of Barcelona's town hall. Seldom do we find ourselves confronted with such an obvious example of the identification of plastic language with faithfulness to an unswerving but limited concept of country.

Josep Obiols (1894-1967). Detail of the decorations of the Hall of Good Government, 1916.
Town Hall, Barcelona.

Jaume Mercadé (Valls, 1887 - Barcelona, 1967) came to Barcelona in 1905, to learn the silversmith's craft, and two years later joined Francesc Galí's school. In 1909 he made a brief trip to Paris and in 1919 travelled to France, Switzerland and Germany with the Vallès composer Robert Gehrard, a student of Arnold Schönberg's. Like all good students of Galí's, he made the requisite journey to Italy in 1921. Between 1917 and 1924 he was a teacher in the Advanced School of Fine Crafts, directed by Galí, and in 1925 had a hand in the major contribution of Barcelona's *Foment de les Arts Decoratives* (Promotion of the Decorative Arts) made to the International Exhibition in Paris. He painted landscapes, mainly of the Tarragona countryside and the environs of Poblet, figures, portraits and still lifes. This is how he expressed his fidelity to his beginnings in a few autobiographical notes that reveal an ever-youthful spirit,

"I believe that the painters of a mature age, like myself, must remain faithful to themselves, to their own concept of painting, though never to the detriment of development. I mean that the painter must develop constantly. Sometimes it does no harm to return to simple topics,

Jaume Mercadé (1887-1967). Portrait of Mrs Rosa Farrés de Mercadé, 1948 (125 × 78). Private collection.

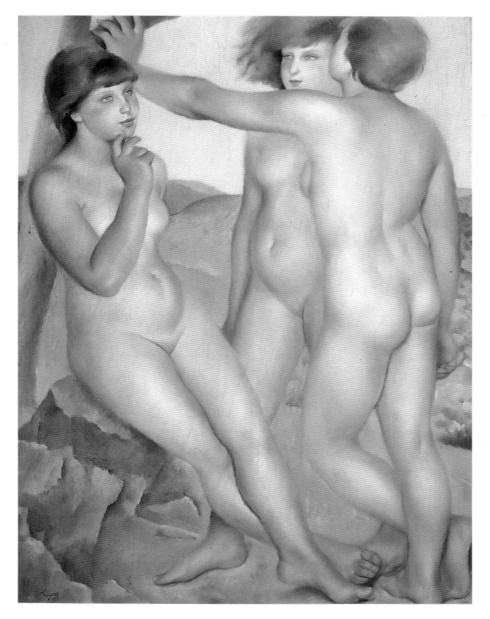

Josep de Togores (1893-1970). The Springtime of Life, about 1927 (129 × 97).
Museum of Modern Art, Barcelona.

especially since those topics nearly always bear within themselves striking truths. So I believe that the saying *renew yourself or die* is true. And as is natural I have no desire to die.''

As for Josep de Togores (Cerdanyola del Vallès, 1893 - Barcelona, 1970), his art appears to embrace certain similar forms, although the painter comes from a very different background. To sketch his biography here would require retracing a colourful, romantic, yet quite interesting career, but I lack the time and space to describe it in full. Belonging to an aristocratic family in the Vallès, he enjoyed a pampered childhood with journeys to Paris and contacts with Belgian art. In 1906 a serious attack of meningitis cost him his hearing. Later he suffered material and family setbacks that left him in very difficult straits. Assisted and encouraged by the criticism of Casellas, Eugeni d'Ors and Josep Maria Junoy, and the special friendship and trust of Aristide Maillol, helped financially by French and German dealers, he eventually won a great success in pre-Civil War Barcelona. His nudes, with their ranges of browns and greys and the soft modelling, like pastel painting, that characterizes his compositions enabled him to harmonize perfectly with Galí, Humbert and Obiols. After the war he turned his talents to the polemical adventure of easel painting on religious subjects, very different from that cultivated by other friends of his.

It has often been said that Antoni Vila Arrufat (Sabadell, 1894 - Barcelona, 1989) was one of the last noucentist painters, although his case stands quite apart from those mentioned above.

He belonged to a dynasty of Sabadell artists begun by his father, Joan Vila Cinca, an academic painter trained between Sabadell and Madrid. Vila Arrufat dedicated himself to easel painting, mural painting on religious and profane subjects, and engraving.

Enric C. Ricart (Vilanova i la Geltrú, 1893-1960), one of Galí's students, belonged to a large Vilanova family and received his early training in local pictorial circles, together with the architect Josep F. Ràfols (Vilanova i la Geltrú, 1889 - Barcelona, 1965). His father, Francesc Ricart, an art connoisseur, befriended such nineteenth-century painters as Josep Beringola, Josep Sugranyes and Estanislau Torrents, who later settled in Marseilles. The development of E.C. Ricart's artistic personality, however, revolved on the Galí Academy, where his companions were Joan Miró and the painter and illustrator Lola Anglada, who had previously studied under Joan Llaverias.

Ricart and Ràfols, together with Miró, were designated by Junoy as belonging to a hypothetical School of Vilanova. Its members, later to include Francesc Domingo, among others, soon afterwards moved on to form part of the Courbet Society, so named by Josep Llorens i Artigas in homage to the great French painter. Togores and Obiols, among others, also formed part of that group for a time. At the end of the First World War, the group broke up, some of its members gradually making the move to Paris. Earlier (during the first months of 1914), Ricart and Ràfols had lived in Florence with another Vilanova painter, Rafael Sala (Vilanova, 1891 - California, 1925), from Munich.

After his stays abroad in Italy and Paris, Ricart rarely moved from Vilanova, where he devoted himself to painting and, above all, wood-engraving, a technique he had learnt in Italy. His subjects are essentially noucentist, countryfolk, fishermen, vineyards and pinewoods, excepting of course the occasional compositions of another kind.

The architectonic baroquism of the First Dictatorship did not completely swamp pictorial noucentism. Here a decisive intervention was made by the collector Lluís Plandiura, friend and protector of the best noucentists. While pseudoacademic Catalan and non-Catalan painters replaced Torres Garcia's mural paintings adorning the Hall of St George in the Palace of the *Generalitat*, Xavier Nogués was decorating, with Jaume Llongueras' collaboration, the office of the mayor of Barcelona and the salon of Lluís Plandiura's house in the Calle de Ribera. Josep Obiols, Manuel Humbert and Josep de Togores, together with Galí, decorated the walls of the National Palace on Montjuic in 1929; their work reveals varying degrees of success.

Meanwhile, however, a great deal had occurred inside and outside Catalonia.

Among the various types of realism, the most interesting example is undoubtedly furnished by the complicated personality of Feliu Elias (Barcelona, 1878-1948). He worked as a caricaturist using the pseudonym *Apa* and as a critic under the name of *Joan Sacs*, a sobriquet taken from Hans Sachs, the character in Wagner's *The Mastersingers of Nuremberg*. He was graduated from the Hoyos Academy. Between 1911 and 1913 he lived mainly in Paris. On his return to Barcelona, he collaborated in editorial ventures undertaken by Santiago Segura and *La Revista*. He was a teacher of art history in the Advanced School of Fine Crafts from 1920 until the general dismissal of the teaching body in 1924 brought about by the dictatorship of Primo de la Rivera. Exiled in 1939, he lived in France until his return to Barcelona in 1947.

In addition to his notable activity as a caricaturist, he designed posters and decorative ceilings. In 1911 he executed a large composition in the form of an allegorical tapestry which the town halls of Móra d'Ebre and Móra la Nova gave as a token of gratitude to José Sánchez-Guerra, ex-Minister of Fomento. On the other hand, the ceilings with erotic themes intended for the decoration of the old Salon Arnau in the Paral·lel of Barcelona, around 1915, represent a total change of conception, though not strictly of technique. His easel painting (figures and still lifes) is very personal and falls within the framework of what we might call magic realism, with a very purified technique at the service of the artist's concept. Nevertheless, he alternated landscapes and decorative ceilings showing little colour and little volume with these pictures.

As a teacher and critic he was very severe and this applied equally to his own artistic creation. He struck up solid friendships with Xavier Nogués and several contemporary draughtsmen, such as Pere Ynglada (Santiago de Cuba, 1881 - Barcelona, 1958), an admirer of Paris, the

Feliu Elias (1878-1948). Antechamber (portrait of Rosa Elias), 1932 (61 × 52).
Private collection.

circus, horses and Far Eastern art; and the prolific Joan G. Junceda (Barcelona, 1881 - Blanes, 1948), of whom Elias painted two allegorical portraits about 1904-1905.

In Barcelona's town hall, between the paintings of Nogués and those of Josep Maria Sert, figures a great allegorical ceiling, painted in a very distinct hyperrealist vein and executed, like the others, around 1928. It is the work of Miquel Viladrich (Torrelameu, 1880 - Buenos Aires,

Rafael Durancamps (1891-1979). Street in Paris, about 1927 (39 × 32).
Private collection.

1956), a restless man interested in all kinds of subjects, although concentrating on the human figure, who often painted on wood as if he were creating an altarpiece. In Madrid, Lleida and especially France, and in a great group for the Hispanic Society of America in New York, he mainly cultivated a Catalan folklorism reminiscent of Feliu Elias' tapestry of 1911. After that, Viladrich took an interest in Moroccan themes and later Hispano-American subjects, the result of a long stay in the Republic of Argentina. Before this final period, during the Spanish Civil War, he painted a strange allegory of a militiaman crossing the Ebro in a boat (MMAB). The contrast with·the realism practised by Feliu Elias is complete and perhaps best summed up by saying that in his greatest works Elias seeks—to good purpose—to express the essence of things, whereas Viladrich is content to present their colourful surface appearance.

Leaving the avant-garde movements for development further below, I should mention the Olot and non-Olot landscape art, which displays a constant exchange between conservative forms, such as those found in the work of Rafael Durancamps, Francesc Labarta (also well

Francesc Labarta (1883-1963). Barcelona City, 1930 (89 × 116).
Museum of Modern Art, Barcelona.

known as a teacher), Joan Vila Puig and Bonaventura Puig Perucho; and other gentler forms, like those employed by Iu Pascual, a Vilanovan transplanted to Olot, as well as other painters from the Galí Academy: Francesc Vayreda, a native of Olot; Ignasi Mallol of Tarragona, who died in exile in Colombia; Marian Espinal and Rafael Benet from Terrassa—the last-named a nephew of Joaquim Vancells very closely associated with Tossa.

Iu Pascual (Vilanova i la Geltrú, 1883 - Riudarenes, 1949) is the paradigm of the middle phase of the Olot school, in which brown tones are juxtaposed with soft greens. The greens resurface later, however, in the painting of Josep Pujol (Olot, 1904-1987).

Rafael Benet (1889-1979). Awning of the Biel Café, Nightfall (Tossa de Mar), 1948-1949 (89 × 116).
Museum of Modern Art, Barcelona.

The persistence of impressionism can be clearly perceived in the paintings of Ricard Urgell (Barcelona, 1874-1924) and Joan Colom (Arenys de Mar, 1879 - Barcelona, 1969), who have left us a number of fine compositions (*Market Interior*, Barcelona Museum of Modern Art, about 1907, by the former and *The Old French Station in Barcelona* of 1911 by the second). The official Barcelona exhibitions of 1907 and 1911, together with that of French art in 1917, in the middle of the First World War, help us to understand this persistence. We find an eloquent example of it in the chronicle of Sandiumenge published in the *Quaderns d'Estudi* or *Studio Notebooks* (June 1917), in which he praised Monet's wonderful *Gare Saint-Lazare*, called "the most elevated work of man's chromatic sensibility," adding,

"I feel almost tempted, standing before this canvas, to speak of virtuosity; such is the knowledge of colour, such the careful technique with which the brushstrokes are juxtaposed, subtler than the iridescence of mother-of-pearl. The objects and the lights, the space and the vapours that float there, the houses and the sky which shines above, the ways of the sun and the construction of the shade, everything sings with the most exquisite and elevated of harmonies; one would say that everything blends together in a permanent miracle which makes visible the marvellous and intimate structure of the air and light."

By way of a coda to the above, we should add here a word of praise for the Nabis, especially Bonnard and Vuillard. The latter had already won a first-place medal at the Barcelona Exhibition of 1911.

Joan Colom (1879-1969). The Old French Station in Barcelona, 1911 (60 × 73).
Museum of Modern Art, Barcelona.

Ricard Urgell (1874-1924). Market, Early Morning, about 1907 (140 × 186).
Museum of Modern Art, Barcelona.

Josep Amat (1901-1991). Seaside (Sant Feliu de Guíxols), about 1942 (65 × 100).
Museum of Modern Art, Barcelona.

Iu Pascual (1883-1949). Autumn, Les Corominotes (Olot), 1916 (54 × 67).
Museum of Modern Art, Barcelona.

Josep Amat (Barcelona, 1901-1991), Rafael Llimona (Barcelona, 1896-1957), and countless others, as happens in so many countries, would later display the persistence of impressionist formulas which shaped great sectors of the painting created in Catalonia, so much so that in 1915 Josep Aragay already raised serious objections to the validity of that plastic expression.

"Impressionism has consisted in a constant preoccupation with the transparency and vibration of light, and has lent painting a new aspect that is neither better nor more beautiful than its former appearances; the majority of modern artists have passed through this aspect, without worrying whether it suited their temperament, as if pictorial art always had to develop under the auspices of impressionism . . ."

Together with the above, we would rank as well those of Galí's students who belong to a more conservative sector, for example Ignasi Mallol (Tarragona, 1892 - Bogotá, 1940), who died in exile after an interesting experience teaching in Tarragona, and Rafael Benet (Terrassa, 1889 - Barcelona, 1979), nephew of Joaquim Vancells and normally active between Terrassa and Barcelona. Living in exile in Belgium because of the Spanish Civil War, Benet produced compositions that are not without interest, still lifes and other works of an intimist nature. He was also a critic, scholar and art teacher.

With these names I shall associate a long series of painters who reached their prime in the 30s, having begun their careers earlier. For example, the group known as the *evolutionists*, a term inspired by a manifesto Torres Garcia wrote (*Art-Evolution* of 1917); Joan Serra (Lleida, 1899 - Barcelona, 1970), and Alfred Sisquella (Barcelona, 1900 - Sitges, 1964) belonged to this group.

Alfred Sisquella (1900-1964). Child, 1929 (50 × 42).
Museum of Modern Art, Barcelona.

Serra created an abundant production (landscapes, figures, still lifes) but was undoubtedly surpassed in his aspirations by Alfred Sisquella, a reserved and intimate man who concentrated his reflection on a number of austere and extremely delicate figures painted around 1929, before embarking on a prolific phase showing a heavier use of oils, in which the figures and still lifes reveal his undeniable technique, perhaps without reaching the levels that his qualities seemed to promise.

Generally, these years mark a period characterized by numerous local exhibitions, by the renovation of the Sala Parés, acquired by Joan A. Maragall in 1925, and the appearance of new galleries or halls of art, such as SYRA, which opened its doors to the public thanks to Montserrat Isern's enthusiasm and tenacity, and Joan Merli's official and private initiatives. Among the critics, we should single out Màrius Gifreda, Joaquim Folguera, Josep F. Ràfols, Rafael Benet and Joan Cortès i Vidal, one of the founders of the evolutionist group, as well as the writers closest to the avant-garde and those who came from earlier periods, such as Joaquim Folch i Torres and *Joan Sacs*.

The taste these men reflect is diversified in numerous expressive labels and idioms. Once again I must point out that in no way am I trying to make a classification that would rival a systematic botanical treatise. On the other hand, inclusion in a single group does not imply equality in the judgment of value, which often proves radically different. Lastly, we are not dealing with watertight compartments and consequently the two great blocks of pictorial

Marian Andreu (1888-1976). Composition, 1937 (22.5 × 27).
Private collection.

Ramon de Capmany (1899). The Terraces of Sants, 1922 (60 × 65).
Museum of Modern Art, Barcelona.

expression or attitude are frequently not separated by unsurmountable or unsurmounted barriers. Moreover, in the course of his life or even at the same time a single artist has been seen to pursue many varied idioms. Limitations of space more than the imperatives of artistic reality may impose simplifications or outlines that do not always correspond exactly to reality, which is indeed often more complicated than conventional divisions.

If we take as a starting point Joan Merli's *33 Catalan Painters* and the review *Art* (1933-1936), we see that these "lists" tend to underline the distinct personalities of individuals, rather than their affinities. However, we see that beyond the pale of Merli's choice there remain many other forms of expression; their existence shows us that the panorama of Catalan artists was much more complicated in fact and that the writer's choice was based on a specific taste, as had already happened in the 20s in the collector Lluís Plandiura's circle.

Outstanding are the landscapes and figures of Marian Andreu (Mataró, 1888 - Biarritz, 1976), Josep Mompou (Barcelona, 1888 - Vic, 1968), Ramon de Capmany (Canet de Mar, 1899), Miquel Villà (Barcelona, 1901), Ramon Calsina (Barcelona, 1901), Pere Pruna (Barcelona, 1904-1977), Josep Maria Prim (Bordils, 1907 - Barcelona, 1973) and Emili Grau Sala (Barcelona, 1911 - Sitges, 1975).

Andreu, who began his career in 1911 with Ismael Smith and Laura Albéniz, under the standard of a decadence Eugeni d'Ors had arbitrarily ranged with noucentism, spent only five

Josep Mompou (1888-1968). The Port of Sóller, 1929 (60 × 73).
Museum of Modern Art, Barcelona.

months with Francesc Galí. Then he worked actively in Paris in the field of enamelling, a technique he had learnt in London, and at the same time met with great success in the French capital as scenographer and illustrator between the two world wars.

Ramon de Capmany, painter and engraver, came to painting in an obviously noucentist milieu. An arch-conservative, he expressed his thinking in the lecture *Some Provisional Considerations on Painting* (1950), in which he combined his admiration for Pascal and the world of Port-Royal.

Josep Mompou went through a preliminary period marked by very refined tones, and a simplification reminiscent of Albert Marquet. Later he developed towards profiles with greater intensity, emphasized by pronounced blue and purple outlines.

The case of Miquel Villà is characteristic of the painters of his generation, although his career exhibits some rather unusual aspects, described in detail by the critic and poet Gabriel Ferrater. Villà was born in Barcelona in 1901. In 1912 he travelled to Buenos Aires with his father and in 1914 his whole family was settled in Bogotá. After various journeys he left in 1922 for Paris, where he stayed until 1930. In the French capital he took part in collective exhibitions and at the same time organized two individual shows in Barcelona in 1927 and 1929. After 1930 he lived in Barcelona and the Masnou. His association with Joan Merli lasted from 1930 to 1936 and involved the acquisition of Merli's entire creative production for the sum of 500 pesetas a month. He passed the Civil War years in various Catalonian towns, eventually emigrated to Argentina where he remained from 1940 to 1943. On his return to Barcelona and the Masnou, he took part in various individual and collective exhibitions. He painted in Paris, Eivissa and Pobla de Segur. In the 50s he also travelled in Italy.

In 1953 he said,

"I prefer painting figures to landscapes, but I cannot do it. My working sessions are very long, and there are many sessions, and there is no model who can stand up to it. On the other hand, I like to place the figures in the open air, and this too is difficult, especially with the nudes ... Along the Catalan coast is the landscape I like painting best. There are two landscapes there: the one we see looking seawards and the one we see looking towards the mountains ... Sometimes a motif I am painting excites me so much that I get up at night and walk through it and touch the trees ... Many of my canvases take a hundred or two hundred sessions and I could continue working on them indefinitely."

Villà gives a highly personal treatment to the intensity of the colours and the whites of his painting and the density of his material.

Ramon Calsina belongs to this series for chronological reasons, even if his style and especially his fertile and singular iconography often lead him into a kind of highly personal surrealism, independent of that of the majority of painters of the same period.

Pere Pruna, endowed with a great decorative sense, protected in his early days by Picasso, practised both mural painting and set design for ballets in the vein of the neoclassical Picasso; this Pruna combined with resonances of the painting of André Derain's best period, which was then quite in harmony with the prevailing mood in Catalonia. On the other hand, Pere Créixams

Miquel Villà (1901). The Stable (el Masnou), 1936 (114 × 162).
Museum of Modern Art, Barcelona.

Emili Bosch Roger (1894-1980). El Paral·lel, 1930 (81 × 100).
Museum of Modern Art, Barcelona.

(Barcelona, 1893-1965), whose work had gone through a very interesting phase in Paris, later tried to recapture subjects of Nonell's that were rather outside their time. Neither Francesc Camps Ribera nor Josep Gausachs succeeded in their independent attempts to escape from Nonell's influence.

Josep Maria Prim divided his creative work between landscapes and flower painting with decorative compositions infused with a nostalgia for the nineteenth century. Likewise Emili Grau Sala, an artist with a sure style and a good illustrator, well received in Parisian circles, painted in a similar mode to very good effect. In the 30s, Antoni Clavé emerged from this formalism, which he then abandoned to work intensively in the avant-garde.

And there were many others like the above artists, each with his own personality and peculiarity and from among whom we might single out here Emili Bosch Roger (Barcelona, 1894-1980).

The upheaval caused by the Spanish Civil War markedly stimulated the field of poster design—inspiring such artists as Martí Bas—but did not give rise to great novelties in painting. Homage was paid in the Barcelona Exhibition of 1938 to Hermen Anglada, alongside Josep Obiols, for example, and Evarist Mora. The previous year, Catalan works of art had been (unsuccessfully) sent to Mexico where, among the paintings in a more youthful spirit, those with Majorcan themes by Joan Junyer stand out in particular, revealing the same characteristics and quality as the works that had figured in the Spring Exhibition of 1936.

I should point out that when the war ended in 1939, two of the greatest historical promoters of noucentism held comparable offices on each of the two conflicting sides: Eugeni d'Ors was

National Head of the Fine Arts in Vitoria and Francesc Galí Director-General of Fine Arts of the Republican Government, with its provisional headquarters in Barcelona.

The great break essentially took place in 1939, with the exile of many artists—along with Joan Merli—and the absolute lack of institutional support for art that had been created in the country previously. To be sure, the galleries of earlier periods continued to exist and other artists continued to create, although there appeared concurrently a kind of persecuting fury and morbid prejudice against everything that could be called new or native.

Certain more or less retrograde theoretical positions had sprung up years before through such critics and painters as Rafael Benet and Feliu Elias, although in addition to these there existed much more radical and extreme points of view. For example, the outlook of the painter and draughtsman Ferran Callicó (Barcelona, 1902 - Nemonde, 1968), author in 1936 of *Art and the Social Revolution*, or the viewpoint defended in *The Adventure of Contemporary Art* (1953) by the painter Francesc Serra (Barcelona, 1912 - Tossa, 1976); *The Discrediting of Reality* (1956) by the Valencian essayist Joan Fuster; *A Spectator Looks at Modern Painting* (1976) by the Sabadell poet Joan Arús; or *Artists or Philistines?* (1976) by Josep Maria Infiesta. Indeed, we might list here many other works, including a book by Joaquim Torres Garcia, which he himself tore into shreds while it was still in manuscript; some notable works of fiction such as *Noba figurassió*, one of many books by Joan Vila Casas (Sabadell, 1920); and the fake biography of a nonexistent contemporary Catalan painter, a fictional friend of Picasso's, *Jusep* [sic] *Torras i Campalans* by Max Aub. Picasso's name, his shadow and light dominate this panorama, as the books of many of these authors—standing for or against the great artist from Málaga—testify.

Ramon Rogent (1920-1958). Window in Portugal, 1947 (46 × 55.5).
Private collection.

A number of recently trained painters and other younger ones would cling to falsely academic formulas, turning art back towards the past as in the days of the First Dictatorship. This ideological involution made possible the success of figures who seemed to come from the past and the advent of young artists who acted out of plastic, and not ideological, prejudices. Hence the fleeting success of the painter Ernest Santasusagna (Barcelona, 1900 - Santa Coloma de Gramenet, 1964) and his pupil Armand Miravalls Bové (Barcelona, 1916-1978), both of them talented, yet holding fast to a conception that seems completely anachronistic to us. In the subsequent years certain characteristics, though not identical, have persisted in the country's portrait painters, stimulated by the presence of others who arrived from throughout the Iberian peninsula. We should recall that the phenomenon is much more widely spread than what art historians usually record and has led in America, for instance, to the rapid growth of such profitable enterprises as Portraits, Inc. Nevertheless, this wave was soon circumscribed within very concrete limits and represented the forms preceding 1936, to which other names subscribed.

On the path towards a total renewal, I should mention a number of young artists who tried to put new art into practice although without making a total break, still difficult or impossible at the time. The Cercle Maillol, founded under the auspices of the French Institute in Barcelona, contributed to this gradual normalization by the granting of scholarships to study in Paris. Other artists achieved such a renewal by widely differing means.

One of the first new groups was headed by Ramon Rogent (Barcelona, 1920 - Plan d'Orgen, 1958), an artist of great fire and ability in getting people together, who worked mainly in Barcelona and London, and died in an accident while on his way to see Picasso with some of his students. Rogent held his first public exhibition in Barcelona with two of Picasso's nephews (sons of his sister who lived in Barcelona with Picasso's mother and was married to a Catalan doctor, Dr Vilató). Another painter, Albert Fabra, also exhibited with them. Years later, one of Rogent's students, Bosco Martí, would complete the decoration (planned by Rogent) of one of the halls in Barcelona's town hall; his work took its place among decorations by the noucentist painters (Galí, Vila Arrufat, Obiols) and Evarist Mora, as well as those commissioned from Antoni Tàpies in 1959 and Albert Ràfols-Casamada in 1982.

Emili Grau Sala (1911-1975).
Masks, about 1935 (130 × 92).
Museum of Modern Art, Barcelona.

THE AVANT-GARDES

I prefer to use the term in the plural because we are dealing with a long process that was frequently interrupted, although for that very reason it deserves our full attention. Seeking literary parallels, we can in fact trace its progress from around 1909. This does not mean, however, that we can find no forerunners of the artistic avant-gardes. Among these forerunners we might include the introduction of the term *futurism*, which has two entirely separate meanings. On the one hand, the Majorcan thinker Gabriel Alomar used it in a lecture given in the Barcelona Athenaeum in 1904 as one of the two elements of a dualist conception of society, opposed to involutionism. On the other hand, long before Marinetti published his *First Futurist Manifesto* in Paris (1909), the term had already been adopted in Barcelona by the plastic artists who in 1907 began the publication of a review called *Futurisme*. Its contents were not without interest, but they had no connection with the forms and tendencies that would arise later.

In fact, the prime mover in introducing the avant-gardes into Catalonia was the dealer Josep Dalmau (Manresa, 1867 - Barcelona, 1937), who settled in Barcelona in 1884, studied under the symbolist painter Joan Brull, was a habitué of Els Quatre Gats and resident in Paris from 1900 to 1905. On his return to Barcelona, Dalmau set up an art gallery in the Calle del Pi, and managed a succession of other establishments until his death. Eugeni d'Ors drew the following portrait of him,

". . . This antiquary appeared one day inflamed with a violent passion for everything that his fellows most detested, in other words, modern art. But on that occasion, for the most radical, innovative and unusual aspects of modern art. I mean for the cubists, the great unsettlers of those days; for the savages among the *fauves*; for the algebraists among the structuralists; for the Sudanese among the cultivators of negro sculpture, unless they should be from the Solomon Islands."

In 1908 he put together an exhibition of Josep Mompou's works, but it was only in 1912 that Delmau would decide to present a group of cubists who had previously never been seen outside Paris and Brussels.

Neither then nor later did he present cubist works by Picasso, who had been struggling in France and Catalonia, creating in Paris at the same time as Braque the purest works of the movement. Nevertheless, Picasso's activity in Catalonia remained on the fringe of local painting trends, although this does not mean his works had not been seen here. In 1909, for example, on his return from Barcelona after a fruitful cubist expedition to Horta d'Ebre, Picasso executed the cubist portrait of his friend and former fellow-student Manuel Pallarès. During the summer of 1910 Picasso and Derain spent several very active weeks in Cadaqués, whereas the following year the great twentieth-century master stayed at the same time as Braque in Ceret in the Vallespir, where Max Jacob, Manolo and Sunyer were also to be found. In the summer of 1912 Picasso was in Ceret again, returning there in 1913, a year in which he spent other stays in Barcelona, Girona and Figueres.

In the autumn of 1911 the critic Josep Junoy, who had been in Paris, Belgium and Holland, returned to Barcelona "excited by the cubists." On 24 October he presented some articles on cubism by Jean Metzinger in the Barcelona daily *La Publicidad*. In the introduction Junoy named Picasso as the initiator of the movement and also mentioned Braque.

Between February and March 1912 we can read in the pages of *La Veu de Catalunya* (The Voice of Catalonia) articles by Eugeni d'Ors (*Xènius*), Joaquim Folch i Torres and Joaquim Torres Garcia on cubism and pictorial structuralism. This was a few weeks before Dalmau opened (on 30 April) a cubist show in his gallery, with works by Metzinger, Gleizes, Marie Laurencin, Juan Gris, Marcel Duchamp, Le Fauconnier, Léger and the sculptor Agero. Max Jacob had been announced as author of the prologue to the catalogue, but it was signed by Jacques Nayral, a figure who intrigued the Barcelona commentators. In fact, it was a pseudonym of Joseph Houot (1879-1914), married in 1912 to Mireille, Gleizes' sister.

Also in 1912, a chapter entitled "From Paul Cézanne to the Cubists" appeared in the book *Art and Artists* by Junoy.

In his article "Conversa" or Chat (7 March 1912), Eugeni d'Ors offered the reader commentary, accompanied by photographic reproductions, on works by Cézanne, Van Gogh and Gauguin, along with allusions to the Douanier Rousseau and the fauves Van Dongen, Matisse and Derain.

For all that, with the exception of Picasso, cubism found no immediate followers in Catalonia, not even in Ceret, notwithstanding the presence and activity of the most significant of the international artists who supported the movement. For a time L'Hospitalet (Barcelona) was home to the Uruguayan painter Rafael Barradas (Montevideo, 1890-1919), a friend of Torres Garcia and promoter of a pictorial movement called vibrationism, with cubist and futurist elements, in which he was supported by the Catalan Àngel Marsà, whom we shall meet again as critic and gallery-owner after 1939. A very interesting avant-garde painter, Joan Sandalinas (Barcelona, 1903), also began to exhibit during the 20s.

We have to wait until the years 1915-1930 to find two Catalan painters as significant to the avant-garde (and as different from each other) as Joan Miró and Salvador Dalí.

We should also remember that the First World War did not favour international communication, although it did encourage the existence in Barcelona of a specific microclimate well worth bearing in mind.

And now let us return to Josep Dalmau. In October 1916 a group of foreigners who had found a welcome in neutral Barcelona were introduced to him in a café on the Rambla. Among them were Francis Picabia, who had arrived in August, Marie Laurencin, married to the German poet and painter Otto von Wätjan, who had arrived two years earlier, and Albert Gleizes and his wife, Juliette Roche, also a painter. There were others, too, such as the Russian painter Sergei Charchune and two English brothers, Otto Lloyd, married to the Georgian painter Olga Sacharoff (Tbilisi, 1889 - Barcelona, 1967), and Fabian Avenarius Lloyd (also known as Arthur Cravan). Dalmau, who had known some of them since the cubist exhibition, and had also organized an individual show for Gleizes, agreed with them to edit a review in Barcelona entitled *391*, a continuation of *291*, edited a little earlier in New York. Only four issues were published in Barcelona (from 25 January to 25 March 1917). Gleizes had left Barcelona in December and Picabia did so when the fourth issue was ready for publication. He arrived in New York on 4 April 1917 and launched a continuation of the review *391*, which was the voice of dadaism and had a very limited circulation. Otto Lloyd and Olga Sacharoff, however, were happily settled in Barcelona and Tossa de Mar (a town to which the whole group made frequent trips). Years later Tossa was transformed into a meeting place for them as well as other Catalan and foreign artists, from Metzinger to Marc Chagall and Georges Kars.

Dalmau continued in the same vein for many years. In 1922, for example, he held an exhibition of Francis Picabia's work, with André Breton writing the foreword to the catalogue. Years before that date, on the other hand, he had organized Miró's first individual show.

Miró was born in Barcelona in 1893. After early studies in Llotja with Modest Urgell and Josep Pagès, he had to interrupt his training until 1912 when he joined Francesc Galí's school; in 1915 he entered the Cercle Artístic de Sant Lluc, where he executed drawings alongside the architect Antoni Gaudí. From his earlier periods, I can only mention two Majorcan landscapes that were shown at the Barcelona Exhibition in the spring of 1911. At the time he had his own studio, together with Enric C. Ricart and Lola Anglada, and struck up friendships with Josep F. Ràfols, a student of architecture, and Joan Prats.

Between 1916 and 1917 he painted a series of landscapes of Cornudella, already mentioned in an earlier chapter. Around October 1917 Ràfols and Miró became members of the Barcelona Athenaeum, where Miró used to go to read Van Gogh's letters. Sometime in 1918, they went to Vilanova to see Ricart, accompanied by Manolo Hugué. At that time Junoy spoke of the existence of a Vilanova pictorial school. Later, in September of the same year, Ràfols and Ricart visited Miró at Mont-roig, where his father had bought the farm that was to become famous as the centrepiece of one of Miró's compositions.

Joan Miró (1893-1983). The Farm (132 × 147), 1921-1922.
The National Gallery of Art, Washington D.C.

The 1918 exhibition in the Sala Dalmau (from 16 February to 3 March) was accompanied by the catalogue bearing a calligram by Josep Junoy, dated December 1917, in a vein that won him great success in France: *forta pictòrica Matèria Impregnada d'una Refractabilitat cOngestionant* (strong pictorial material impregnated with a congestive refractability), the name Miró appearing here as an acrostic. Victòria Combalia has made public the letter of congratulations that Santiago Rusiñol sent Miró on the occasion of the exhibition in the Sala Dalmau.

Coinciding with an exhibition of his work, Miró wrote a letter to Ricart in February 1918, considered as a sort of manifesto by many,

"I believe that after the grandiose French impressionist movements which sang of life and optimism, and the post-impressionist movements, the courage of the symbolists, the synthesism of the fauves, and the analysis and dissection of cubism and futurism, after all that we shall see a free Art whose 'importance' will lie in the resonant vibration of the human spirit. This modern analytical trend will have brought the spirit to a radiant Freedom. Since the spirit will be strong and free, if, when we start a canvas, we still commit the error of wanting to rally around some flag, instinct will take over, despite our very selves; like Cézanne who wanted to do 'serious painting' and win 'medals' at official exhibitions.

"I am anxiously waiting to savour the futurist writings against outmoded Rome and its moonlit nights. Down with all sentimentalism, sickly light of the half-moon, weeping sunsets in canary yellow, and clouds of dark red feathers, twilights, sun rays gilding a mountain for a last few moments. Down with all that, made by crybabies! Let us be real men. Let's transplant the primitive man to ultramodern New York, inject his soul with the din of the subway, of the 'el', and may his brain become a long street of buildings 22 stories high. . ."

Miró had joined the Courbet Society, which was to enjoy only a brief existence, because with the end of the war, the artist members would gradually begin to move to Paris. The last to arrive there was Miró, for he wanted to be sure he could hold an individual exhibition in the French capital. It actually took place from 28 April to 14 May 1921 in the La Licorne gallery, with a catalogue prefaced by Maurice Raynal, one of the most prestigious critics of the day. Miró's first stay in Paris coincided with the sojourn Torres Garcia made there on his way to the United States. Miró went to meet him at the Gare d'Orsay, arranged for him to put up at the Hôtel de Rouen, where Ricart and Dalmau also had rooms, and would accompany him throughout his stay, save on one visit to Picasso's house which seems to have proved fruitless.

On the other hand, Miró's first visit to Picasso, which took place some months later, was an unqualified success. Picasso had visited the Miró exhibition and bought a picture of a Spanish dancer, speaking very favourably of Miró to the dealer Léonce Rosenberg. When Miró first went to visit Picasso, he was somewhat bewildered by the variety of styles and conceptions of plastic expression the Málaga artist was then using, so much so that Miró would later remark that he felt as if he had visited a female dancer with different lovers. Nevertheless, Picasso's cordiality and humanity helped to overcome all his prejudices; it was the start of a solid, lasting friendship. Evidence of this was the presence of a Miró self-portrait in Picasso's private collection.

In one of their conversations, we know that Picasso said that "in Catalonia, passion and heroism are lacking because that's what art is." This was a concept similar to that of the *valour* to which Miró had referred in 1918.

In 1922 Miró occupied a studio in Paris along rue Blomet, next to that of André Masson, who years later would be one of the assiduous visitors to Tossa de Mar. Between Mont-roig and Paris Miró painted *The Farm*, which he exhibited in the Salon d'Automne of 1922 and was acquired by Ernest Hemingway three years later. The American writer compared it in Miró's œuvre to the leading role that *Ulysses* represents in James Joyce's literary production. For many years the painting remained in the house that Hemingway owned in Cuba, built on the model of a Catalan *masia* or farm.

Miró's art was one of the favourite subjects of the group that edited the review *L'Amic de les Arts* or Friend of the Arts (1926-1929) in Sitges. J.V. Foix, Sebastià Gasch and Salvador Dalí contributed various articles to the review. In 1928, for instance, Dalí published an article in the review from which the following paragraphs are taken,

"Joan Miró . . . knows how to separate the yolk from an egg cleanly, so that he can appreciate the astronomical course of a comet's tail. To the line, to the point, to slight distortion by tautening, to figurative significance, to colours, Joan Miró restores their purest and most elemental magic possibilities.

"By way of automatism and superreality, Joan Miró's paintings lead us to appreciate and discover, approximately, reality itself, thus corroborating André Breton's reflection according to which superreality is contained in reality and vice versa."

In 1934 J.V. Foix was the author of an article included in a number of the review *Cahiers d'Art* devoted to Joan Miró,

"'How can you possibly fit Joan Miró's painting into the Catalan tradition?' a critic disillusioned with my country asked me recently. He asked *me*, me, a firm supporter of Maurras' saying, '*Everything that is ours is national*'. It would be hard for me to admit that a temperament of such Catalan stock as Joan Miró's could produce a painting foreign to the sensibility typical of the people of our country.

"Yet in Joan Miró not only is there no deviation, but also those who accuse him of heresy with respect to traditional painting (who are the same people who brand as heretics with respect to painting in general all those who dare to express themselves plastically in a manner different from the official, academic and temporary norm) forget that the pictorial tradition, like the literary, has not been established through the communication of manual skill passing from father to son, but rather through original 'revelation' in the philosophical sense of the word.

Joan Miró (1893-1983). Painting, 1934 (97 × 130).
Miró Foundation, Barcelona.

"All the essential plastic peculiarities of Catalan painting, all that is most native in medieval Catalan painting, already pointed out by objective criticism and certain essayists, you will rediscover in Joan Miró's painting. If he has assimilated some of the temporary characteristics of international painting, his plastic formulation has been effected with such originality that it would be quite difficult for us to establish which trend he was backing. More venturesome, however, than the oft-quoted famous painters of the Romanesque and Gothic schools, who characterize one of the most beautiful periods in Catalan art, he has given his creations a vigour so personal that not only does he sum up all the attempts at independent creation observed during the historical formation of Catalan painting, but he also surpasses the aims of such attempts in order to offer us, within the framework of European painting today, an independent expression and a unique personality.

"Place the pictorial creations of the European artists who can be said to belong to a particular school side by side and you will realize that one thing is certain: only Joan Miró maintains an undeniable racial and temperamental reality. And if you make a comparison with the outstanding works of the most important periods of Catalan painting, you will discover the reason for it: the same root preserved and nourished down the centuries by certain local characteristics (in geographical order): simplicity, clarity, objectivity, plasticity and—let us not reject the paradox—REALISM."

One of the most important works in the year 1934 was the great ceiling that simply bore the title *Painting*. It belonged to Joan Prats, friend and admirer of Joan Miró since the days of the Cercle de Sant Lluc.

It is impossible to sum up in a few words Joan Miró's extensive œuvre throughout the subsequent years or the wealth of literature it has inspired.

When Eugeni d'Ors exhibited Joan Miró in 1950 at the seventh Madrid Salon, along with works by Dalí and the *Dau al Set* group, he made this assertion, "The first artist, sir, to have a personal cosmos. Who in contemporary art enjoys that in the same proportions as Joan Miró?"

Josep Llorens i Artigas, the critic who gave the Courbet Society its name, later became an exceptional ceramicist. He and Miró collaborated on a number of great murals all over the world, executed in places as distant as Baltimore, New York and Osaka. One of the first and most important of their joint creations was the walls called *The Sun* and *The Moon* overlooking an open space in the headquarters of UNESCO in Paris. Two of Joan Miró's letters to Llorens form a very valuable document in helping us to understand the terms of their collaboration,

[31 August 1956] "We talk a lot with Sert (Josep Lluís Sert, architect) . . . About UNESCO he said that he has given you a great deal of technical advice that you must take careful note of because of its importance. We talk of the execution of my project, it must be very courageous and powerful so that the light does not eat it up and it is not overshadowed by the enormous masses of architecture surrounding it. He says I must carve to a depth of four to five centimetres so that the lights play on the line I am making; otherwise it would disappear and lack force, a vital element in these murals. I think so, too.

"I know that with all this I am confronting you with new and difficult technical problems, but I know that you will solve them. All this offers parallels with the theatre. I remember my experience in 1933 when staging *Jeux d'Enfants* (Children's Games. I planned one part of the ballet with the dancers wearing tights of every subtle shade of colour. In rehearsal I saw that all these subtleties disappeared in the powerful spotlights and that I should use potent primary colours. The UNESCO mural has to be handled in the same spirit, so that it is not destroyed by the surrounding environment."

[26 September 1956] "Before leaving for Palma, I visited Güell Park. You live near it and I should like you to go there when you are in Barcelona. It has all been made with a very keen feeling for the noble material and suggests a great affinity with what we are doing. The two entrance towers are decorated with rectangles as I very often do.

"The walls are distorted and uneven, giving the park great vitality. We do not need to worry if, *without deliberately seeking it*, firing gives us the same result *naturally*, which will form a striking contrast with the rigidity of the architecture.

"What you really must see, and which will give us ideas for hollowing out and making the great red circle, is this. On your way to Güell Park, before entering by the main gate, and keeping to your left on the same pavement, in a very out-of-the-way corner of the terrain, facing a bourgeois tower, lies a great circle hollowed out of the actual stone of the terrain, with several little steps leading up to one of the extremities of the park.

"You would also find it very interesting to see the great Romanesque frescos in our Museum of Montjuic."

Miró's interest in Gaudí is quite understandable if we bear in mind the chromatic value of some of the architect's works, for example the facing of the Batlló house façade and many features of Güell Park, among them the keystones of the cloister under the great square.

In order to understand the permanent features of Joan Miró's vast production in the years after 1925, we must take into account the counterpoint existing in his paintings between the emphatic outlines of the large figures in flat tones, often indicated by black lines, and the constant chromatic vibration of the grounds.

In 1956 Miró made Palma de Mallorca his main residence, but it was in Barcelona that he launched the Foundation that bears his name, open to the public as the *Centre d'Estudis d'Art Contemporani* (Centre for the Study of Contemporary Art) in 1975. On his death another institution was set up in Majorca, where he had always had family ties. It was the *Fundació Pilar i Joan Miró* (Pilar and Joan Miró Foundation), established legally in 1981.

Salvador Dalí died in 1989 in Figueres, where he was born in 1904. It is no doubt highly significant that his long career finished in the same city in which it had begun. We must not forget, however, that between these two moments he spent many years residing by turns in three very different places, namely by the sea in Portlligat, which lies in Cadaqués, and in Paris and New York, as in well as Barcelona, Madrid and Púbol.

After a preliminary period of pictorial apprenticeship in Figueres, his father sent him to Madrid in 1922, to the Real Academia de San Fernando, so that he could obtain the highest existing title in the fine arts.

This resembles Picasso's father's intention when he, too, sent his son to Madrid. In neither case, however, did the result turn out as their fathers had wished.

Dalí lived in the Students' Residence and made friends there with such significant figures as the Aragonese film director Luis Buñuel, the poet Federico García Lorca (a native of Granada), and the poet and writer José Moreno Villa, although the atmosphere he came up against in the Academy was too conventional. In spite of the conformity, the period in Madrid brought him his first contacts with surrealism.

The paintings of this period recall works by contemporary Italians. Like them, Dalí turned to the Mediterranean and settled in Portlligat as the main source of his inspiration. In an earlier chapter, I have already transcribed a number of his texts with descriptions of the landscape he would remain faithful to throughout his life. As a complement, I should now add remarks by J.V. Foix in the article "Dalí at Portlligat," published in 1935,

"The majority of his pictures lay bare the mystery of our geology. Without the landscape of Cabo de Creus there could be no easy interpretation of the most personal Dalinian subjects. When Dalí was interested in soft bodies (limp watches, ulcerous flesh), he was always a man of the seaside. Whether they are fossils or alive, the bodies in Dalí's painting have a fishlike quality. The circle of his imagination is enclosed like a cove with no outlet."

This landscape is combined with the inexhaustible inventiveness of Salvador Dalí, who would often play with the illusionist effects of *trompe-l'œil*, so much so that he has influenced many aspects of world advertising design and played a part in ballet decor and set design for the cinema, from Buñuel to Hitchcock and Walt Disney.

We must bear in mind that in Dalí's case, he set himself up in the centre of a one-man show, proving himself an exceptionally imaginative writer of prose as well.

This allowed him to stay in touch with French surrealist circles and the Sitges group that published *L'Amic de les Arts*. Nevertheless, at other times this popularity was counterbalanced by Dalí's predilection (and that of some of his colleagues) for provocation, a predilection that, in the long run, led inevitably to one breach of friendship or another after it had brought him to the peak of popularity.

In Sitges circles, he managed to convince Gasch and Montanyà (though not J.V. Foix) to sign jointly a typically provocative piece called *Manifest Groc* or Yellow Manifesto (1928), a less intelligent text than many others, saved by not only its ingenuity but also its imaginative richness.

Along with literature, Dalí's painting passed from a cubist phase to another classicizing one, before reaching a magic realism in pictures that combine natural elements with other fantastic features; these compositions were often shown in Paris and the series of Barcelona galleries run by the tireless Josep Dalmau, one of his most convinced promoters.

On 6 October 1934 Salvador Dalí was in Barcelona, where he had opened an exhibition in a hall managed by Josep Dalmau in the Llibreria Catalònia. Dalí, frightened by the revolutionary events taking place at that time in Catalonia and the Asturias, fled to France, foreseeing the future convulsions that two years later would give rise to the Spanish Civil War (1936-1939). In this state of mind, he planned a composition in 1934 that was called *Soft Construction with Boiled Beans*. After a brief stay in the United States (November 1934 - February 1935), Dalí, starting from a preparatory drawing, pursued the idea and painted a canvas (finished at the beginning of 1936) he called *Premonition of Civil War*.

In his fantastical autobiography, *The Secret Life of Salvador Dalí*, written in 1942, Dalí descibes the completed canvas as follows, "In this picture I showed a vast human body breaking out into vast excrescences of arms and legs tearing at one another in a delirium of autostrangulation. As a background to this architecture of frenzied flesh devoured by a narcissistic and biographical cataclysm, I painted a geological landscape that had been uselessly revolutionized for thousands of years, congealed in its 'normal course.' The soft structure of that great mass of flesh I embellished with a few boiled beans, for one could not imagine swallowing all that unconscious meat without the presence (however uninspiring) of some mealy and melancholy vegetable."

Once the Civil War was over, the desire to introduce himself into official Spanish and American circles led Dalí to create a colder and more conventional painting, of which many examples exist. This does not mean to say that he stopped taking an interest in the outside world and the most significant scientific discoveries.

In the last years of his life Dalí linked his fate very closely with that of a strange figure, Gala (Helena Dmitrievna Diakonova, died 1982). In 1917 Gala had married the French poet Paul Eluard, whom she divorced in 1932, although she had been living with Dalí since 1929. Gala's correspondence with Paul Eluard (until 1948) constitutes a document that is very illustrative of this strange and complicated ménage. There are also numerous articles and books by Salvador Dalí, whose real and imaginary contents blithely mingle fact and fiction. Indeed, this confusion forms the basis and essence of Dalí's painting. If that is its main attraction, it is also no less a reason for the reader's or the observer's perplexity.

One notable action on Dalí's part was his vindication of Antoni Gaudí's art as a sculptor and architect, coinciding with Joan Miró's championing of Gaudí's painting.

On the other hand, his appreciation of Meissonier belongs to the past and verges on the paradoxical. As for Marian Fortuny, Dalí formulated his praise of the artist in 1963 in this paradoxical form with a touch of irony, "In a dress coat painted by Fortuny, in a piece of the fabric in *The Spanish Wedding*, thousands of microscopic *Battles of Tetuan* are contained. I managed to get one of the most talented abstract expressionists, Willem De Kooning, to have a look at it. He was struck with admiration by a fragment of *The Spanish Wedding*.

"The art critic Michel Tapié is already planning a book in colour in which the patches and brushstrokes of Fortuny will be amplified and analyzed scientifically as in the study of chromosomes, thanks to electronic microscopes. . ."

Finally, the most serious and honest assessment made by Dalí is found in a comparative table published as an appendix to *Diary of a Genius* (1964-1974), which mentions some important ancient and modern painters, with Dalí awarding Vermeer his highest classification.

Salvador Dalí (1904-1989). Soft Construction with Boiled Beans; Premonition of Civil War, 1935-1936 (100 × 99).
Philadelphia Museum of Art.

I must mention other events prior to 1936-1939. On the one hand, Torres Garcia's relations with Catalonia continued. The painter exhibited once again in Barcelona on various occasions, in Antoni Badrinas' gallery in the Diagonal and elsewhere. He also kept up a correspondence with friends like Joan Agell, who had welcomed him in New York. Torres Garcia wrote to him in 1928 to describe his conception of the painting he was working on at the time, while in touch with the international avant-gardes, especially those of Holland and Paris, where he took up residence once again between 1926 and 1932:

"... Moving on, then, to the second thing, that which motivated the picture, it can be said in a word: plastic values.

"Plastic values set freely in play, and a proportion, a rhythm of the line, and tones in agreement with all that.

"Rather like music, and here the line would be, for example, the melody and the colour the accompaniment. The chords, those points of coincidence between the two elements.

"For me, today, the main element in a picture would be the proportion, and afterwards the rhythm, and if, after the above is well set out, that represents something, so much the better. That, my good man, seems to me to be the greatest step that painting can take today, to return to its centre, to what it must be *in itself*, which would be the return to classicism in whatever it may hold to be essential. It does not differ, then, from music, nor architecture, not (I venture to say) from what literature, and even more, poetry, ought to be. Cubism tried to resolve this problem but, for lack of ability on the part of those who attempted it, was unable to do so. At all events, it did a lot of good, in the sense of advancing towards the construction of something conceived, and above all cleansing painting of its maximum aberration, which is the imitation of reality in the manner of a photographic apparatus. I have tried to create what could be called *pure* painting and I use the term in the philosophical sense. And my great task from now on will be to introduce *humanity* into it, not to convert this pure painting into an inhuman painting."

In 1930 he added,

"I've already said, I think, in another letter, that since I've been in Paris, I've painted more than a thousand pictures. I'm also doing a vast amount of writing. I've got around so that I know all the intellectual world here, as well as the critics and dealers, and I've already had nine exhibitions and organized three collective exhibitions, and formed a group of Latin-American artists and another international group (*Cercle et Carré*). . . Faith can never die in me. And above all, faith in painting. Every day I work with more enthusiasm than ever. And I see that I am approaching something that offers me repose. . ."

During his stay in Paris, Torres Garcia kept in touch with Catalan painters of the younger generations, some of whom, such as Pere Daura (Barcelona, 1896 - Rockbridge Baths, Virginia, 1976), settled later in the United States, and Pere Créixams (Barcelona, 1893-1965), bought pictures from him. In the French capital he also renewed his acquaintance with the painter and sculptor Juli González (Barcelona, 1876 - Arcueil, 1942), who tried to make up the friendship between Picasso and the Uruguayan artist. Juli González' personality was focused on the field of sculpture, so I shall not mention him here. In addition to him, we must not forget his brother Joan (Barcelona, 1868-1908) and the former's daughter Roberta (Paris, 1909 - Arcueil, 1976), who formed a notable family group that started with Concordi González, Barcelona metal-worker, father of Juli and Joan, and was completed by their sisters, Pilar and Lola.

We know that in 1932 Torres Garcia, still in Paris, maintained ties with the Barcelonan painter, critic and poet Josep M. de Sucre, whom we shall meet again after the Civil War as president and promoter of the Maillol Circle, in his native city.

At the end of that year, faced with the international crisis, he moved to Madrid, where he stayed for more than a year. Finally, he returned to Montevideo in 1934, a city from which he never moved again, and where he completed a new chapter in his life as man and artist.

I have already pointed out that the political and environmental circumstances after 1939 caused a major interruption in Catalan artistic life until the younger generation could rebuild it on a firm foundation.

Although some of the important artists of the pre-war periods managed to struggle on one way or another, the fact remains that the Second World War, following close on the heels of the Spanish Civil War, continued to impose a general closure of frontiers and make circulation, both physical and cultural, very difficult.

Although some signs of improvement appeared, with such painters as Domènec Olivé Busquets (Barcelona, 1892-1959) and Pere Gastó (Barcelona, 1908), real change did not come about until 1945 with the end of the war, and I think it is pointless to seek other explanations, such as the internal development of the country or the political regime, or artistic idioms in general.

Domènec Olivé Busquets (1892-1959).
The Two Friends, about 1951 (149 × 164).
Museum of Modern Art, Barcelona.

As one can imagine, we lack a global perspective; furthermore, the proximity of events and the excess of material and information make it difficult to identify the major lines of development, although this does not mean that such lines do not exist.

The Maillol Circle, established by the French Institute in Barcelona in 1945, was the first milieu favourable to the thawing of cultural exchanges in the plastic arts. I must emphasize the stimulating role played by its two successive presidents, the expressionist painter Josep M. de Sucre (Gràcia, 1886 - Barcelona, 1969), who headed the Circle until 1963, and the critic and intellectual Arnau Puig (Barcelona, 1926). They were accompanied by Xavier.Valls (Barcelona, 1923), the only one of the Circle's founders to travel to Paris, where he settled permanently. His landscapes and still lifes possess a refined and gentle subtlety.

The French Institute's scholarships enabled other artists with extremely varied styles to visit and stay in France. Some of them produced a rather naive art, as was the case with Joan

Xavier Valls (1923). Still Life with Pears and Oil Lamp, 1986 (92 × 73).
Museum of Modern Art, Barcelona.

Brotat and Josep M. Garcia Llort, who later spent some time in the United States, and Josep Guinovart. Others moved towards surrealism or informalism, not to mention those who favoured expressionism and the adherents of geometricizing compositions. New galleries along with a few of the old that had come to life again offered this younger generation the opportunity to show their work at either individual or collective exhibitions. Of the latter, I must mention, among others, the October Salon, inspired by Víctor M. d'Imbert and held from 1948 to 1957; the May Salons, begun as a continuation of the former; and the efforts of both the Association of Modern Artists and the Club 1949. The upsurge of more or less ephemeral groups occurred not only in Barcelona, but also in many other Catalan cities; the Sílex Group in Lleida and tha Gallot Group in Sabadell, for example. As for examples outside Catalonia, the endeavours of Eugeni d'Ors in Madrid, the *Academia Breve de Critica* (Brief Academy of Criticism) and *Sálon de Los Once* (Salon of the Eleven), deserve special mention.

Owing to the great number of examples, I can mention here only several specific cases.

In the first place, that of the group called *Dau al Set*, which had as forerunner two ventures undertaken in Sarrià in 1946. The oldest was the publication of the one and only issue of the review *Algol*, on the initiative of Joan Ponç and the poet Joan Brossa. Enric Tormo, Arnau Puig, Jordi Mercadé and the sculptor Boadella also collaborated on it. Brossa introduced the group to J.V. Foix, who arranged to present their work in the excursionist centre Els Blaus, with compositions by August Puig, Joan Ponç, Tort and Boadella. The exhibition was visited by Antoni Tàpies and Modest Cuixart, who very soon joined the group. As well as visiting J.V. Foix's house, Joan Ponç put them in touch with some artists who met in a Sant Gervasi establishment called *La Campana* (The Bell), where they made the acquaintance of a Dominican painter, Jaime Colson.

Later Enric Tormo introduced Joan-Josep Tharrats (Girona, 1918) to the group. He was the son of a writer associated with many cultural ventures in Girona. The meetings continued in the house of J.-J. Tharrats where, in 1948, they decided to published a review, which had the blessing of Joan Prats, collector and friend of Joan Miró from the Sant Lluc days.

The idea coincided with the convening of the first October Salon. In 1949 Tharrats also introduced to the group the critic and poet Juan-Eduardo Cirlot (Barcelona, 1916-1973), who was especially interested in surrealism and had a book on Joan Miró soon to be published.

In fact, the review *Dau al Set* served as a temporary force—temporary yet very interesting—binding seven artists of widely differing approaches; united in 1948, they started dissociating themselves from the group successively since in 1950. The group finally dissolved in 1953, when Joan Ponç moved to Brazil, where he would remain for ten years. The magical surrealist style, partially inspired by Klee, Miró, Max Ernst and Kandinsky, and the stimulating personality of Joan Ponç formed its powerful, though ephemeral, binding agent.

The spectral and hallucinatory world of Joan Ponç was summoned up in a special way by J.V. Foix in the collection *97 notes on Ponçian fictions*, illustrated by Joan Ponç and published in Barcelona in 1974. I would like to insert here several extracts giving a very complete idea of the world in which the group's conversations and activities took place,

"It must be admitted that, rightly or wrongly, Joan Ponç made absolutely no concessions to taste. He did not chase after the sunlit beauty of an attic terrace, nor confine himself to any accepted laws; he did not even claim to improve on the lodgings of an Andalusian serving girl. Alogical and unreasonable—in appearance?—one would say that he takes leave of his senses to reach the shade where the stars tear themselves to pieces. He is not an 'artist,' in spite of being both a hard-working plastic investigator and a craftsman with his ears pricked up. He is neither a realist, nor—God forbid!—a 'modernist.' Neither is he a smart 'avant-gardist'. On the contrary, there he is, completely alone like a snail on a balcony rail, with its head half out of its shell and its feelers up. Or like a bishop stretched out on a plot full of bones, twisted bits of iron and manuscripts containing treatises on perspectives. . .

"No calendar marks the seasons in these Ponçian landscapes in the form of a polychrome zebra under a sky full of clouds turning green, with bloodstained stars and moons torn apart by their anxiety to make haste. . .

Josep Maria Garcia Llort (1921). Homage to the Soda-Water Drinker, about 1956 (94 × 120).
Private collection.

"Blessed is he who advises us to paint freed from the obsession with isms, asymmetrical blues and the flattery of the self-satisfied! A painting, as nearly the whole world already says, is either good or it isn't, be it realistic or idealistic. Be your own avant-garde. If you see with courage, dodge the bulletins of dehydrated art, the notarial pages of the age of red Garibaldi blouses and mustard in tin cans. . .

"Neither an art nor a literature of the avant-garde exists. Multiple avant-gardes exist in the rhetorical and plastic explorations which, once given expression, enter the academy, the museum or the asylum for hopeless cases. Picasso, Miró and Dalí, contemporaries and almost of an age, do not resemble each other at all in their works, and even oppose each other. To hear them speak, the three of them consider themselves as avant-gardists. There was a bellicose futurist avant-garde of Italian inspiration which turned cubist in France and disintegrated into dadaism in Switzerland. There was a 'surrealist' (esoteric, alchemical) avant-garde in France which was not far short of becoming occult. The avant-garde in Germany was starchy and expressionist. . .

"Let us pass, at a gallop, from dadaism to pop art, art-pop and arte povera without having had time to know their bureaucrats nor those who equip them. Experiments, trials, tests of great interest for following the development of plastic values, and the permanence of true worth in each one of these solid experiments. The lucid, the impetuous, the intelligent, the irresolute, the false, the fantastic, the phlegmatic, the frivolous, the one who does not know where he's going and the inconstant are there, frankly and without duplicity or fraudulent and fleeting, as in every period. *But do not take up your brush on Saturdays; you will come up against the witches. We are in the kingdom of the eye in a land where the eye replaces the heart. Everything is contemplated wearing a nightcap and bed socks, and in one direction only.*

"The man who told you: 'I'm a futurist, it's in my blood,' soon afterwards proclaimed himself a pre-Max Ernst 'surrealist' and contemporary, as though it were nothing at all, of the artist who discovered the junk room: Chirico. With thirty thoroughly enjoyed siestas behind him, he believed he was an existentialist from birth. Now, he has turned structuralist and spatialist simultaneously and—oh, Mother of God, I can't believe my ears!—concrete. He is usually the buttons of the group of bearded members of the antibeards, '. . . *de petits bourgeois irrités*,' as the Parisian *Magazine littéraire* puts it. With very little canvas and a pair of crutches with thick rubber tips, at the far end of a dark narrow passage. . .

Joan Ponç (1927-1984). Roser, about 1952 (164 × 97).
Private collection.

"When the avant-gardes wither away in the texts of their proclamations—oh, those moving adorable autumns!—the 'neos' are born: neo-impressionism, neo-classicism, neo-futurism, neo-dadaism. They are often a parody of those trends and in some cases their caricature. The 'neos' are, without doubt, the victims of an atavism. Or they are atavistics pure and simple. They lived on the crumbs and ruins of antiquity. They move backwards, convinced that they are advancing, and reply when everybody knows the answer...

"To be *in* the avant-gardes does not mean to be *of* the Avant-garde or even to be 'avant' at all. The Yankee, Brazilian, Slavic or Hindu hour does not exist. Everyone is his own avant-garde when everyone is the same. Man, by birth, is universal and polyglot, and at the same time, deep-rooted and monolingual, which does not mean monolithic. Nevertheless, do not put too much trust in those who change styles like Pepeta at the dyer's who changes her hair style to be in fashion. The grandmother at *can Faci* used to say that fashion, you have to make one for yourself. Development or change of style must be the result of necessity or imperative speculation. Or revitalizing procedures or putting theories into practice. What is not allowed is the initiative taken by the impotent. Every artist may have 'his styles.' Seen and contemplated from afar, in space and time, they are converted into a single, personal one. Hybrid styles, if there be any, do not count for the responsible critic. When night falls, he hears the subtle sounds that come from who knows where, the rustling of the leaves, the song—or lament—of the late birds and the frogs, and those distant voices which, although he can never quite tell whether he knows them or not, he likes to hear, and the shrillness peculiar to solitude."

The ghostly, green portrait of Roser (Ponç's first wife) enables us to evoke visually the full force of the artist's plastic language, which is complemented by a very important group of graphic works.

Modest Cuixart, *working within a range of warmer tones, let himself be seduced by this world*, as recorded in 1955 in some explanatory remarks by Arnau Puig. They were spoken in Terrassa shortly before the ephemeral foundation of the Taüll Group which proposed the inclusion of these and other artists,

Modest Cuixart (1925). The Circus, 1950 (115 × 195).
Private collection.

Joan-Josep Tharrats (1918). Memory of Kyoto, 1970 (131 × 164).
Art and Technology Foundation, Madrid.

"Like the rest of us, Cuixart struggles in a confused and turbulent atmosphere, where the first thing to do is to seek to find and recognize oneself. Modest Cuixart wants to achieve this by means of the purest thing: the pictorial material and craft, but not that craft which was required before, when all that counted was the ability to adapt oneself to the object; rather the craft that allows the continuous creation of a whole series of ranges that produce pleasant sensations and capture our retina. Naturally, all this draws him towards a new and more beautiful play of colours, although the artist tries to flee, with a somewhat tragic longing to cling to this optimism that escapes him against his will."

In the following years his surrealism drifted towards fantastic faces, then went through an informalist phase in which a luxurious-looking material using a golden crimson predominated, before returning to figuration in his last days.

J.-J. Tharrats, apparently guided more by a cosmic world, with black, whites, pinks and reddish tones, came to abstraction along other paths, experimenting with different techniques, including *maculatures*, impressions comparable in some ways to monotypes, for we must not forget that he, like Enric Tormo, often practised the graphic arts.

In his text *In Order to Understand Tharrats* (1963), Alexandre Cirici had this to say, among other things, ". . . Tharrats is a man capable of adhering to ideas, things and people in a sensitive way. That is the source of the two great qualities I most appreciate in him: his enthusiasm and his generosity. Not only has he lavished his enthusiasm on his own enterprises, such as *Dau al Set*, the Salón del Jazz and the Taüll Group, but he could always be counted on to take up the cudgels on behalf of new art. The writer will always be grateful to him for an enthusiastic and disinterested collaboration on his own enterprises, such as the lectures at the *Club 49*, the A.A.A., the May Salon, the Gris Prizes, the Museum of Contemporary Art and the F.A.D. School of Art."

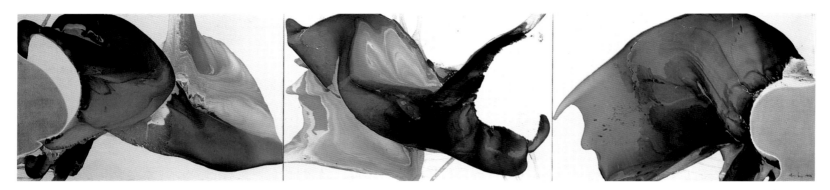

August Puig (1921). Your Blues (Homage to Juan-Eduardo Cirlot), 1974 (96 × 436).
Museum of Modern Art, Barcelona.

The museum mentioned was a project promoted by Cirici in 1960, the forerunner of other ventures, some successful, others not.

On the fringe of the group, although he took part in the exhibition of *Els Blaus* (The Blues) in 1946, is the painter August Puig (Barcelona, 1921), associated to some extent with the non-figurative forms of various German painters. The quality of his material and the lyricism of some of his works make it understandable that he kept up his relations with Cirlot, in whose homage he dedicated the great triptych entitled *Thy Blues*.

Tàpies, who earlier had used thick coats of pigment and samples of collage between 1945 and 1947, embraced the poetic language of *Dau al Set* between 1948 and 1954, while retaining astral themes with Mirónian associations and geometric schematizations. Nevertheless, around 1950 he began at the same time to bring to his canvases the magical realist drawing characterizing many of his sketches of former years. It was in the years 1950-1951 that Tàpies made his first stay in Paris, where he met Picasso.

The year 1953 saw the appearance of maculature techniques, also employed by other artists, until from 1954 on there predominates in Tàpies' work the use of great thick coats of paint along with the frequent recourse to very sober ranges in which extremely short lines and patches stand out in contrast. In 1953 Tàpies' first exhibition was held in New York; this great cultural centre advanced the diffusion of his art in America and furthered his knowledge of many of the most important American artists.

He won one of his first public prizes at the third Hispano-American Biennial in Barcelona (1955) and the prize of the Carnegie Foundation in Pittsburgh in 1958 was also significant. In 1959 he executed a series of pictures for Barcelona's town hall and in 1990 a group of ceilings for the Tàpies Hall (also known as the Hall of the Four Chronicles) in the Palace of the *Generalitat*. It is impossible to recall in detail the vast volume of Antoni Tàpies work. Among the first groups executed in Switzerland, I would single out the soffits for two walls in the library of the Advanced School of Commerce in St Gall (1962).

In addition to the extensive bibliography on Tàpies, we should bear in mind that the artist himself has written many articles, separately or in collections, and an autobiography, *Personal Memorial* (written for the most part in 1966 and published in 1977). All these materials help us to recapture his personality and his thinking. The *Introduction to the Aesthetic of Antoni Tàpies*, prepared by J.-F. Ainaud i Escudero in 1986, comprises an anthology of Tàpies' writings completed by an interview.

Here are several extracts,

J.-F. A.: "Are there definite phases in your work? In the affirmative, what are they?"

A. T.: "Yes, there are some writers, no doubt you've read them, who have been pointing them out. Broadly speaking, I would say that I began in a very intuitive way, using some deliberately provocative forms influenced by the language of the dadaists. It was at that time that I made sketches with bits of paper stuck on to them and scratches with crosses, etc., like the first pictures I showed at the First October Salon held in Barcelona in 1948. It was a comparatively brief period, but I consider it important in my career as a whole.

"Then came the moment when I began to take greater interest (with the influences peculiar to every young painter) in the techniques and some of the formulations of surrealism: all that business of psychic automatism, the symbols of the unconscious. . . and I was also refining my painting, perhaps ridding it of the most provocative elements and seeking rather the subtleties that oil painting could still provide. Nevertheless, little by little I realized that I was shutting myself up in a sort of dead end, as I think many other people who have studied surrealism have realized. Surrealism had a great theoretical and literary value; it was essentially a very literary movement, but surrealist painting, on the other hand, really had very little to offer. And I had the intuition that I had to get away from it and begin to experiment with the specific language of painting, that is, forms and colours (at this time abstract art obviously had some influence on me), after which, there is a third element, perhaps the one I have delved into more deeply than other artists in the pictorial community. It is the expressivity that textures have, in other words the roughness, the qualities of the materials on their own, so that they already constitute a language. To sum up, after the dadaist phase, I moved on to a more refined surrealism and afterwards I embarked on what has come to be known as 'informalism.' Then I greatly developed this material aspect of the pictures, and the relief of the picture acquired such importance that in the end I was actually making three-dimensional objects. In a way, you could say that they were also sculptures, of course. Perhaps it was more a question of objects, making good use of actual objects or deforming them in some way, or fitting various objects together. And this whole

Antoni Tàpies (1923). Imaginary Garden, 1949 (96 × 129).
Ludwig Museum, Cologne.

block of things could be placed inside this informalist tendency which links up with Arte Povera. All this has been said since, of course. When I was working, I knew nothing about these labels!

"Recently I have been entering a final period, let us call it that, in which rather than speculating by using materials close to the earth, I have experimented with more watery, more liquid materials. If one could explain the expressivity of painting with the elements traditionally considered as making up the Universe (earth, air, fire and water). . . There was a time when I worked a great deal with earth and now I work a little more with water and even with airy things, with space. In short, all these elements are things that are interconnected, it is not that I have ever broken with any of them. . . Now I also work with fire when I make ceramics."

J.-F. A.: "Which elements or factors of each stage in relation to the preceding and subsequent one do you think are permanent, which develop and which change?"

A. T.: "As a permanent element I would probably have to consider the work's content more than anything else. I have always seen all this search for form in terms of specific ideas, specific feelings, specific emotionalities that I would like to express, and therein there may indeed be a more stable continuity. It is not a question of repeating the same thing over and over again, because obviously what I have been doing down the years is to continue incorporating new data into my development in an attempt to go more deeply into the knowledge of reality. And then there *is* development, but with many permanent features that are the basic coordinates of every artist and every person working in the world of culture. Basically there is always a desire to seek forms that help us to understand reality and, in accordance with this understanding of reality, to adopt an ethical attitude in life as well. . .

"This general label of a 'material' stage bothers me somewhat, because actually I've made many materials. That is to say, I've speculated with the quality of the surface more than with the thickness of the material, as I've told you before, and sometimes I've respected the message that is inherent in certain materials: a scrap of newspaper, a piece of wood, a bit of sandpaper, a handful of earth. . . Every material expresses something. So when they talk of the 'stage of the material,' it sounds as if I had only made those thick materials, that I more or less invented them, mixing powdered marble with a synthetic glue or a synthetic varnish. . . But this only happens in a few pictures; alongside those there are many that have no 'material.' In other words, the critics sometimes overgeneralize and perhaps they also want to overrefine their assessments. . .

"As for me, I have hardly ever made a marked change or an abrupt break; it has always been a question of thinking hard about things and then developing slowly. Perhaps the most

abrupt change was realizing (this happened around 1951-1952) that I was coming to a dead end with 'surrealist' painting and that the images created were literary ones, that is, they could be explained with words; the plastic effect remained very much in the background, and that has happened to many painters who have remained with this purely literary form of expression. A typical example in our country is Dalí. . . On the other hand, I have managed to emerge from the expression of academy techniques, because they have some—shall we say—philosophical connotations that make you keep on expressing a message characteristic of another period, if you use them."

In many other texts, in *Personal Memorial* for example, Tàpies tries to express his concept of a basic non-figurative language and place it in relation to the world of the Far East, something which he and several other writers, among them Lluís Permanyer, have considerably emphasized.

Let me quote several passages from the above-mentioned book by Tàpies;

"Starting from those (let's say 'Epicurean' and 'musical') pictures from my earlier period, by dint of going more deeply into the analysis of space and plastic materials, I arrived at surprising results. It was a paroxysmal work on the ever more complicated structures (specifically pictorial or 'abstract' as people called them then) with which the works were composed. Dividing them up, impressing them with baroquism, subdividing them, almost destroying them, to the most extreme degree, suddenly and strangely the work was again given the appearance of a united, smooth, monochrome mass, but one which now consisted of a surface composed of millions of elements or accidents. This gradually gave me the idea of forming it by mixing real corpuscles of all kinds: sand, coloured soils, whiting, powdered marble, hair (once I even used the powdered hair accumulated in the remains of my daily shave) and threads, rags, scraps of paper, etc., which seemed to me to give the impression of a cosmic accumulation of millions of elements. And it was then that I went from discovery to discovery, especially when one day all this quantitative hotchpotch of elements effected a qualitative change and was not only transformed into unified (or smooth, as I have said) surfaces, but also converted, in my eyes, into walls, into *'tàpies'* [mud walls].

"'St   destiny of a name,' as Ivon Taillandier remarked later. What strange, mysterious circums   fortunes, what long mazes had conjoined to lead me into this situation? It is c   omes from nothing and that logically, inevitably, all the earlier influe   riences had brought me there. Was it perhaps the culmina-tion   chisme' which abounded throughout the world at the

Antoni Tàpies (1923).
Decoration of the Handels-
hochschule Library, St Gall.

time? Was it a reaction in order to flee the legion of amorphous dissolutions that were coming into fashion? Was it weariness with an over-abstract art and an exit leading to the concrete? Perhaps for someone else this discovery would have passed without attracting too much attention, it would not have brought out all the consequences that excited me in the years to come and which produced an immediate echo throughout the world as well. Yet how could it help drawing attention to me! A strange fate, indeed, that of my name, which made me recall the remarks of an esoteric colleague, Salvador Aulèstia, about the influence our names have on us.

"A great many suggestions can emanate from the image of the wall. Separation, confinement, the weeping wall, evidence of the passage of time, clean, serene, placid, airy surfaces and others that are tortured, old, decrepit, etc.

"Nevertheless, anyone who believed that all my efforts were concentrated on creating walls would be mistaken. The need to use earthy materials has constantly hounded me from my first youthful works. Even from those beginnings I always stressed the expressivity of the *texture* of painted forms. I thought that the 'quality' of everyday oil painting already had its own connotations, a fact that made me very excited. I cannot say that I am the only artist to have discovered this, but I would be unfair to myself if I did not say that I explored this third aspect of plasticity (colour, form, texture) far more than anyone else in the artistic world at the time.

"Now I see that the characteristics of that textural quality were the response to a great many complicated intentions, but nobody should think that I discovered them at the time, let me say it once again, by applying a specific method. No, they were the result of constant dialectical study and experimentation. What were these intentions of mine? I was attracted more than anything by the 'new visions of the world' provided by scientific discoveries in all kinds of fields. Nor should anyone believe that with my recent textural qualities everything was reduced to reproducing or suggesting molecular structure, atomic phenomena, the world of the galaxies, microscopic images, etc., however important they might be. For me, and as I saw was the case with many thinkers who stimulated me, Physics and Mathematics were inseparable from Philosophy and Ethics, and even Politics. . . And it is not surprising that more general, meditative allusions emanated from my materials. There was the symbolism of dust, with a whole series of implications: 'To become one with the dust, therein lies the profound Identity; that is, the inner Identity with the depths between man and nature!' (Tao Te King); the symbolism of ashes, earth, or mud, the clay from which we come and to which we return; the symbolism of the grains of sand which seem to demonstrate the fragility and insignificance of our life, and also the solidarity that comes from thinking that all the differences between us are the same as those existing between one grain of sand and another, in other words, none.

"I may also have been led in that direction by the desire to provide a cosmic theme of meditation and reflection on the beauty of the infinite combinations of the forms and colours of natural materials, like the contemplation devoted to the rugosities of Japanese ceramics used in the tea ceremonies."

In the collection entitled *The Practice of Art*, Tàpies reproduces the 1967 essay "The Game of Knowing How to Look," in which he says, among other things,

"How can we look cleanly, without seeking to find in things what we have been told there ought to be in them, but simply what is there?

"Here is an innocent game I suggest we play.

"When we look, we normally see what is around us: four things (sometimes very poor things) seen only from above, in the midst of the infinite.

"Take a look at the simplest object. Take an old chair, for example. It seems to be quite unimportant, but just think of the whole universe it comprises: the hands and sweat cutting the wood that one day was a sturdy tree, full of energy, in the middle of a leafy forest on high mountains, the loving work that constructed it, the weariness it has alleviated, the grief and the happiness it has born, in great halls or the dining rooms in poor districts. . . Everything, everything takes part in life and has its own importance! Even the oldest chair has inside it the initial force of those saplings that rose from the earth, out there in the woods, and will continue serving to give heat on the day when, converted into firewood, the chair is burnt in some hearth.

"Look, look thoroughly! And let yourselves be completely carried away by everything the look offers you that vibrates in your inner being, like a concertgoer in a new suit with his heart open, in the hope of simply listening to the music in all its purity, oblivious of the fact that the sounds of the piano and the orchestra must needs represent a specific landscape, or the portrait of a general or a historical scene, as was often the sole task required of painting.

"Let us learn to see like the concertgoer. In music there are sonorous forms composed within a section of time, in painting, visual forms composed within a section of space.

"It's a game. But playing a game does not mean doing things 'just because'. And as in every children's game artists, too, do not do things 'just because'. Playing. . . playing as children, we learn to become grown-ups. Playing. . . playing, we make our spirit grow, we amplify the field of our vision, of our knowledge. Playing. . . playing, we say and hear things, we awaken the dormant one, we help the ignorant one and the one whose vision has been obstructed.

"When we look, we must never think what painting (like everything in this world) 'has to be', or what many want it to be and nothing else. Painting can be everything. It can be a flash of sunlight in the midst of a gust of wind. It can be a storm cloud. It can be the traces of a man through life, or a kick (why not?) that says 'enough!' It can be a soft breeze at dawn, full of hopes, or a sour breath coming from a prison. It can be bloodstains from someone wounded, or the song high up in the blue or yellow sky of a whole town. It can be what we are, the today, the now and the always.

"I invite you to play, to look attentively. . . I invite you to think."

We now come to Antoni Clavé (Barcelona, 1913) whom I have mentioned above with respect to his earlier periods.

Antoni Clavé (1913). Now and Then, 1987 (197 × 256).
Museum of Contemporary Art, Barcelona.

Easily accessible in the pre-war works which derive from the Romanticism of Emili Grau Sala; more personal in the Spanish Civil War posters.

Exiled in France and on very good terms with Picasso, Clavé produced works that no doubt suggest certain similarities to the Catalan master in the series of great personages called *of the Kings*, although later he turned to abstraction and collage, especially after having spent a second period in Japan in 1986 (his first stay dating from 1972). Among many others, I must also mention his journey to Prague with the School of Paris group in 1946, which enabled him to establish interesting contacts with Czech painters and collectors.

During his travels and exhibitions he never ceased to keep up his associations with Catalan circles.

Joan Vila Grau (1932). Stained glass window (detail).
Baptistery of the Church of the Virgin of Peace, Barcelona.

Francesc Todó (1922). Bicycles, 1958 (60 × 120).
Private collection.

The field of abstraction has other representatives in many different materials. For example, the painter Joan Vila Grau (Barcelona, 1932), who took a personal interest in the creation of stained glass windows, unlike other artists who confined themselves to designing *cartoons* or models.

Josep Grau-Garriga (Sant Cugat del Vallès, 1929), a painter by training, began to work in the sphere of tapestry production, temporarily managing Tomàs Aymat's factory in Sant Cugat del Vallès, promoted at the height of noucentism by Francesc d'A. Galí. Later, encouraged by Jean Lurçat, who was in Sant Vicenç, near Perpignan for a time, he was intensely active in the field of textile experiments in various countries.

Josep Royo (Barcelona, 1945) began by collaborating with Joan Miró in the creation of tapestries but later executed more personal and original works. He settled in Tarragona in 1971.

Among the many artists taking part in the October and May Salons I might mention Francesc Todó (Tortosa, 1922), with an abundant and interesting œuvre that includes engraving, poster design and mural painting.

Together with a varied and intense range of colouring, violent at times and toned down at others, this artist's structuralism confers on him an affinity with architects from Barcelona and Madrid, such as Oriol Bohigas and Fernando Chueca. I should like to reproduce a few remarks by each of them, "He is the painter of a living society who works unselfishly, silently, who keeps on serenely entering into his own daily work. . . Todó is the man who sets to work with a sincere and honest craftsmanship" (Bohigas).

"Sometimes it seems to us that the look frees itself from the will and begins to wander of its own accord, devoted with delight to its contemplative task. That is what happens when it encounters this delicate mass, reiterative, agile and obsessive at one and the same time, that forms the fabric of Todó's paintings. . . In the same way that the natural landscape is revealed to us by painters, this other, ever more obsessive landscape has its interpreter and discoverer in Todó. So his pictures again take an aesthetic trajectory (discovery of the framework and the plane), but coming from somewhere else. Going to meet it with contemplative tenderness and not with destructive violence. . . It is a world struggling between integration and disintegration. Todó is a born integrator" (Chueca).

Montserrat Gudiol (1933). Woman with a Paintbrush, 1989 (64 × 53).
Private collection.

We have seen how the critic Juan Eduardo Cirlot (and let us not forget that he was a poet), a member of the *Dau al Set* group, turned his attention to surrealism and later informalism. His personal activity in the fields of poetry and symbology, and a great receptiveness to artistic sensibility led him to take an interest in two very different painters, namely Montserrat Gudiol (Barcelona, 1933) and Amèlia Riera (Barcelona, 1934).

Montserrat Gudiol, endowed with an innate gift for drawing, was trained alongside her father, a great specialist in Gothic painting and promoter of the Galerías Layetanas where the

October Salons were held. A close observation of altarpieces and a knowledge of Antoni Tàpies' works executed in the style of magic realism may have helped her to contrast different facts on which to form an opinion. Cirlot and, more recently, Corredor Matheos have devoted monographs to her. The former takes an interest in her iconographic aspects and proposes a division of her work into pictorial periods beginning in 1950.

Amèlia Riera began in a group that was very active within the Cercle Artístic de San Lluc, promoting the *Ciclos de Arte de Hoy* (Cycles of the Art of Today) and MAN or *Muestra de Arte Nuevo* (New Art Show). Daniel Giralt Miracle has emphasized her use of ranges of black (with blue-greys and purples) and a "type of composition bound up with the symbolism of death and all its connotations. With funeral themes and materials, she builds a world that is sometimes Romantic and sometimes truculent." In a 1962 exhibition Cirlot spoke of Amèlia Riera's "dramatic and elaborate works" and the rhythms crossing her pictures at right angles. In a monograph dated 1990, Maria Lluïsa Borràs writes about the 1986 series of *Triptychs*, including the one entitled *Someone Has Shed a Tear of Blood*.

Maria Lluïsa Borràs has assessed Amèlia Riera's pictorial phase around 1986 as her *prime*, and going beyond pure contemplation (to which I often prefer to adhere), she states,

"Everything seems to be a kind of invitation to penetrate timeless abodes to discover (we know not which) the mystery of life or the silences of death.

"Her work does not deal exclusively with death, the Black Lady nor the holocaust, but it conveys and reveals to us man's supreme frustration. . .

"Once accepted, the invitation to penetrate these frozen abodes, the enigmatic and sumptuous circles, the silent and perverse world of the painter, produces the uncomfortable sensation of having arrived too early or too late to take part, as voyeurs, in a splendid ceremony-cum-spectacle, in a celebratory rite with erotic pleasure as the supreme good and death as the final destiny. . .

"The painter also establishes the pre-eminence of the inner world over the sensible universe and confirms that the true life is inevitably the absent everlasting. . ."

Amèlia Riera (1934). Someone Has Shed a Tear of Blood (Triptych), 1986 (196 × 386).
Art Fund of the Generalitat de Catalunya.

Carles Mensa (1936-1982). Men and Ape, 1981 (132 × 114).
Museum of Modern Art, Barcelona.

The two above-mentioned painters took part in the *Salones Femíninos de Arte Actual* (Feminine Salons of Present-day Art), which included, among others, Maria Assumpció Raventós and Aurèlia Muñoz, the former, with extensive graphic works, and both of them producing important examples in the field of tapestry making.

Many different artists took part in the *New Art Show* celebrated in 1964 and the six founders of the *Cycles of the Art of Today* exhibited separately in the same year. Among them was Carles Mensa (Barcelona, 1936-1982), who in his last years turned to a hyperrealism akin to certain aspects of the Valencian artists of the *Equipo Crónica*, although his was a more acrimonious temperament. Francisco Valbuena and Lluís Bosch, members of the same circle, have remained faithful to informalism.

To complete this heterogeneous panorama we have to retrace our steps and mention some of those trained in Ramon Rogent's studio, which produced artists of widely differing personalities who took part in several of the Salons of May and MAN. In his early periods Jordi Curós (Olot, 1930) showed considerable expressive power, while remaining permanently faithful to figurative painting, a treatment that he later executed in perhaps a more accessible and conventional manner. Josep Roca-Sastre (Terrassa, 1928), for example, was one of Rogent's students and later a teacher in his own studio. Roca-Sastre has mainly devoted himself to Barcelona subjects, which include themes taken from Gaudí's architecture, although he has also practised many different genres, especially still lifes of a consistency that could well be called stony.

Among the list of those who held scholarships from the French Institute in Barcelona more or less associated with the Cercle Maillol, I might mention Maria Girona (Barcelona, 1923), Albert Ràfols-Casamada (Barcelona, 1923) and Joan Hernández Pijuan (Barcelona, 1931). Their plastic language remains totally independent although each of them has passed through various phases. Ràfols, son of a painter in the traditional style, is also a poet, and perhaps as a result preserves a basically lyrical kind of painting. One of his public works is the decoration of four vaults in Barcelona's town hall representing the four seasons (1982). The painter used there soft colour ranges in which sky-blue predominates. On the other hand, Hernández Pijuan (a prolific graphic artist) exhibits sharper contrasts with large black areas. He was one of the promoters of the so-called Grup Sílex (Flint Group).

Jordi Curós (1930). All Three, 1952-1953 (116 × 89).
Museum of Modern Art, Barcelona.

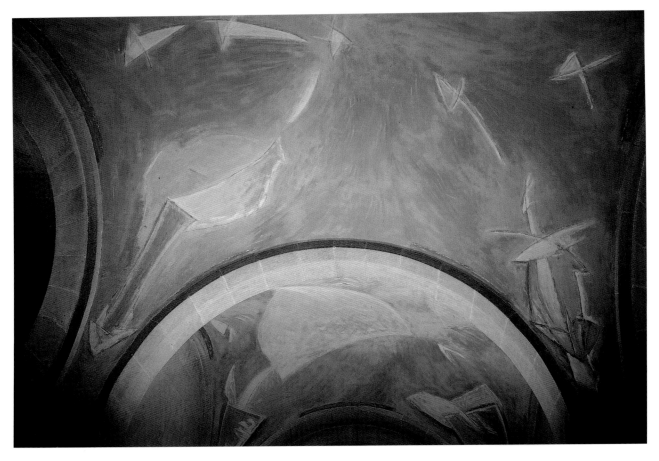

Albert Ràfols Casamada (1923). The Four Seasons, 1982.
Mural painting on four vaults of the Public Information Bureau, Town Hall, Barcelona.

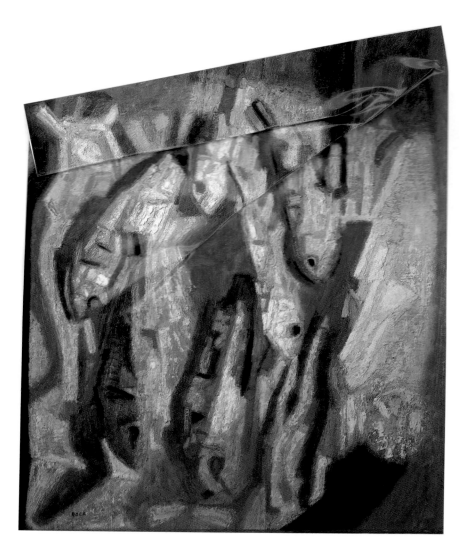

Josep Roca-Sastre (1928).
Still Life with Herrings,
1961 (100 × 81).
Private collection.

Meanwhile, the Lais Group, inspired by the critic J.R. Masoliver, was also active in Catalonia. Outstanding in the group were the painters Manuel Capdevila (Barcelona, 1910), Enric Planasdurà (Barcelona, 1921-1984) and Josep Hurtuna (Barcelona, 1913-1978), who, like Planasdurà, remained faithful to abstract painting while Capdevila continued to execute figurative compositions. Hurtuna produced an excellent graphic œuvre.

Like Jaume Mercadé, Manuel Capdevila was both silversmith and painter. His painting can be classed as expressionist. It was dominated by landscapes, although there exist a few portraits, among them a very important one of Masoliver.

In 1955 the third Hispano-American Biennial of Barcelona assembled works by many artists of widely differing importance; the same year saw seven of these artists come together to found the self-christened Taüll Group, which included (in addition to Tàpies, Tharrats and Cuixart) Josep Guinovart (Barcelona, 1927), Jordi Mercadé, known as *Jordi* (Barcelona, 1923), Marc Aleu (Barcelona, 1922) and Jaume Muxart (Martorell, 1922).

Joan Hernández Pijuan (1931). Flowers on Yellow and Black, 1988 (192 × 168).
Private collection.

Josep Guinovart (1927).
The Abstract Painter, 1952 (180 × 47).
Private collection.

Josep Guinovart has pursued a long career, going through many different phases. A great worker in painting, graphics and ceramics, he is also author of such interesting montages as *Contorn-Entorn (Outline-Setting)* in the Maeght Gallery, Barcelona, 1976-1977, later transferred to and expanded in the Barcelona Museum of Modern Art. Originally, it simulated a kind of fantastic wood. Although he was acquainted with informalism, his world falls between Miró's and Picasso's, and has been expressed ironically in works like *The Abstract Painter*. Josep Corredor Matheos has written at length about his artistic production, as have previously Cesáreo Rodríguez-Aguilera and José María Moreno Galván.

In 1965 Alexandre Cirici tried to classify him in the new realism school, similar to that of some Valencian painters, although one of the most popular products of pop art in Catalonia, the external decoration of the TIPEL factory in Parets del Vallès, comes much closer to it. It was a joint work by the painters Eduard Arranz-Bravo (Barcelona, 1941) and Rafael Lozano-Bartolozzi (Pamplona, 1943), the latter settled in Barcelona in 1963 and was associated at first with Robert Llimós (Barcelona, 1943) and later with Arranz-Bravo. A first version of the painting of the factory was executed in 1971, but the current one (which is reproduced here) is the second, finished in 1988. Francesc Artigau (Barcelona, 1940) lives and works in a similar milieu.

Jordi Mercadé, son of Jaume Mercadé, spent a long time in Paris, pursuing an expressionist idiom comparable to that of the painter Joan Abelló (Mollet del Vallès, 1922).

Aleu has remained within the framework of a geometricizing language comparable to that of some French and Hispano-American artists.

Muxart, boasting a large pictorial production, has often used forms with softened outlines that display a predominance of blues and whites and touches of deep colours, closer to abstraction than informalism.

Francesc Vila Rufas (*Cesc*), born in Barcelona in 1927, has been very active as a draughtsman, although he has also worked as a painter, showing quite refined sensibility. His brother Jordi (Barcelona, 1924) is essentially a muralist and designer of stained glass windows. In the former fields, he participated in 1976 in the decoration of the Archive of Accounts in the Palace of the *Generalitat* in Barcelona. Other artists had already taken part between 1954 and 1960 in the decoration of the Barcelona residence known as Llars Mundet, one of the first unconventional post-war creations in Barcelona.

Jaume Muxart (1922). Galileo Galilei, about 1971 (146 × 114).
Museum of Modern Art, Barcelona.

At the Eigth October Salon, held as part of the Third Biennial, we also find Antoni Guansé (Tortosa, 1926), settled in Paris for many years, and Romà Vallès (Barcelona, 1923), one of the pioneers of informalism in Catalonia, who has also devoted himself to an outstanding teaching career.

Between 1971 and 1980 a group of artists representing *conceptual art* in Catalonia stirred up a public debate in which, among others, Ferran García Sevilla (Palma de Mallorca, 1949) took part as the school's moving spirit. Tàpies, Cirici and Imma Julian expressed opposing views. As often happens in this kind of polemic, a clearcut conclusion was not reached, as in many other cases that have arisen in the international field. For all that, I cannot help mentioning it, although the materials and products of conceptual art do not belong to the field normally classed as *painting*.

The more immediate present and the prospects for the future raise problems that largely exceed the limits of this book. Hundreds of local and international exhibitions, with such manifestations as the Kassel Documenta, and the art fairs of many cities, create a complicated panorama in which expressive idioms and manners are repeated everywhere.

Eduard Arranz-Bravo (1941) and Rafael L. Bartolozzi (1943).
Tipel Factory, 1971 (renovated in 1988). Parets del Vallès.

Names such as those of Joan-Pere Viladecans (Barcelona, 1948), Albert Porta, known as *Zush*, Pep Trujillo, Tomàs Gómez and Sílvia Gubern may be mentioned along with the authors of montages (Muntadas, Miralda, Benito and, earlier, Jordi Pericot), who stand outside the traditional framework of pictorial techniques.

Among present-day painters I might mention as very characteristic the Majorcan Miquel Barceló (Felanitx, 1957), who defines himself as "an overseas Catalan," with an international career after Documenta VII of 1982; Barceló is also highly successful in Barcelona, where he executed the decorations for the dome of the Flower Market Theatre. Victòria Combalia has shown personal handling of genres which would be conventional in other artists (figures, landscapes, still lifes). In statements made to Francisco Calvo Serraller in 1990, Combalia points out the following, "Tàpies has always been a very important influence on my work, and so has Miró. Tàpies had this aspect of working on the surface and is, for me, very close as a painter."

For all that, I think that we can see no more than a partial recognition of contacts or relations in these statements, for even if what Combalia says about her interest in the material is true, the two artists are widely separated conceptually. And I say this in recognition of the very different personality expressed in Barceló's painting, thinking of the degree of personification he achieves in his landscapes, which is almost an epic element. This, paradoxically, would place him in a line running through Courbet and the best of Martí i Alsina in pictures of storms at sea. I do not see this character as being far removed from the Atlantic storms or the deserts of Mali as Barceló handles them. In my opinion, this shows that in the tremendously diverse world of painting, we can recognize human motivations that have more in common than one would imagine.

Miquel Barceló (1957). Storm on the Atlantic, Vila Nova de Milfontes, 1984 (103 × 150).
Private collection.

BIBLIOGRAPHY

LIST OF ILLUSTRATIONS

BIBLIOGRAPHY

The three sections of bibliographic information provided here correspond to the usual practices of Skira editions (books, articles and catalogues). Given the extensive bibliography concerning Catalan painting of the last two centuries and especially the abundance of works devoted to the figures of Picasso, Miró, Dalí and Tàpies, we have chosen to focus attention on a number of basic titles only. Furthermore, we have disregarded special editions created by artists in collaboration with writers. Likewise, due to the great number and variety of articles, specifically in art criticism, in the corresponding section we have restricted ourselves to a partial list that includes the most important reviews and periodicals. Finally, as for catalogues, which we have arranged conceptually, we have taken care to list those of the principal exhibitions. Nevertheless, we must bear in mind that alone the city of Barcelona boasts over one hundred galleries which organize collective and individual exhibitions throughout the year and produce such a number of catalogues that it is impossible for us to mention all these publications here. The best and most thoroughly documented catalogues provide ample bibliographic references which the interested reader may wish to consult to complete our own selection.
The following bibliography was prepared by Joan-Francesc Ainaud i Escudero.

BOOKS

AGUILERA CERNI V. *Julio, Joan, Roberta González.* Barcelona, 1973.

AGUILERA CERNI V. *Porcar.* Fernando Torres Ed., Valencia, 1973.

AGUILERA CERNI V. *Arte y compromiso histórico (sobre el caso español).* Fernando Torres. Ed., Valencia, 1976.

AGUSTÍ A., RAILLARD G., TÀPIES M. *Tàpies. Obra completa, 1943-1960.* Fundació Antoni Tàpies — Ed. Polígrafa, Barcelona, 1988.

AGUSTÍ A., FRANZKE A., TÀPIES M. *Tàpies. Obra completa, 1961-1968.* Fundació Antoni Tàpies — Ed. Polígrafa, Barcelona, 1990.

AINAUD J. *Eugeni d'Ors i els artistes catalans.* Reial Acadèmia Catalana de Belles Arts de Sant Jordi, Barcelona, 1981.

AINAUD I ESCUDERO J. F. *Introducció a l'estètica d'Antoni Tàpies.* Ed. 62, Barcelona, 1986.

ALCOLEA ALBERO A. *Ramon Casas.* Ed. Ausa, Sabadell, 1990.

AMIR X. *Els pintors de la Costa Brava, avui.* Palafrugell, 1982.

ARAGAY J. *Itàlia. Poemes.* Barcelona, 1918.

ARAGAY J. *La pintura catalana contemporània, la seva herència i el seu llegat.* La Revista, Barcelona, 1916.

AREÁN C. *Arte joven en España.* Publicaciones españolas, Madrid, 1971.

ARENAS C., CABRÉ N. *Les avantguardes a Europa i a Catalunya.* Ed. La Magrana, Barcelona, 1990.

ART CATALÀ. ESTAT DE LA QÜESTIÓ. Vè Congrés del CEHA, Barcelona, 1984.

ARTÍS A. A. (SEMPRONIO) *Minutero barcelonés.* Ed. Barna, Barcelona, 1963.

ARTÍS A. A. (SEMPRONIO) *Retrats de Ramon Casas.* Ed. Polígrafa, Barcelona, 1970.

ARTÍS A. A. (SEMPRONIO) *Aquella entremaliada Barcelona.* Ed. Selecta, Barcelona, 1978.

ARÚS J. *Un espectador ante la moderna pintura.* Ed. Ariel, S. L., Barcelona, 1958.

ASPECTES DE LA CULTURA CATALANA ACTUAL. Ed. Franciscana, Barcelona, 1961.

ATENEO DE MADRID. CUADERNOS DE ARTE. Publicaciones españolas, Madrid (Collection).

AUB M. *Jusep Torres Campalans.* Tezontle, Mexico City, 1958.

BARQUET N. *Eugenio d'Ors en su ermita de San Cristóbal.* Ed. Barna, 1956.

BARROS T. *Los procesos abstractivos del arte contemporáneo.* La Coruña, 1965.

BASSEGODA B. *El pintor D. José Masriera.* Barcelona, 1915.

BASSEGODA J. *El Círculo del Liceo. 125 aniversario. 1847-1972.* Círculo del Liceo, Barcelona, 1973.

BENACH M. *Pablo Milá y Fontanals, gran figura del romanticismo artístico catalán.* Vilafranca del Penedès, 1958.

BENET R. *Joaquim Vayreda.* Junta Municipal d'Exposicions d'Art. Barcelona, 1922 (facsimile ed., Barcelona, 1975, preceded by "Estudi preliminar de l'obra artigràfica de Rafael Benet" by F. Fontbona and F. Miralles).

BENET R. *Bosch-Roger.* Galeries Dalmau, Barcelona, 1931.

BENET R. *La figura patricia y el arte de Joaquín Vayreda.* Ed. Aymà, Barcelona, 1943.

BENET R. *Xavier Nogués.* Ed. Omega, Barcelona, 1949.

BENET R., BENET J. *Impresionismo.* Ed. Omega (Historia de la pintura moderna), Barcelona, 1952.

BENET R., BENET J. *Simbolismo.* Ed. Omega (Historia de la pintura moderna), Barcelona, 1953.

BENET R. *Joaquim Vancells. El hombre y el artista.* Ed. Figuras y Paisajes, Barcelona, 1954.

BENET R. *Sunyer.* Barcelona, 1975.

BERGA I BOIX J. *L'estudiant de la Garrotxa.* Barcelona, n.d.

BERTRAN I DE AMAT F. *Del origen y de las Escuelas.* Barcelona, 1908.

BLANCH M. *Manolo.* Preface by Joan Ainaud. Ed. Polígrafa, Barcelona, 1972.

BLUNT A., POOL P. *Picasso. The formative years. A study of his sources.* Studio Books, London, 1962.

BOHIGAS O., CASTELLET J. M., RODRÍGUEZ AGUILERA C. *Tres ensayos polémicos sobre la pintura de Todó.* Preface by F. Chueca. Joaquim Horta, Ed., Barcelona, 1961.

BOHIGAS TARRAGÓ P. *Apuntes para la historia de las Exposiciones Oficiales de Arte de Barcelona.* Barcelona, 1945.

BORJA VILLEL M. J. *Fundació Antoni Tàpies.* Introduction by Miquel Tàpies. Fundació Antoni Tàpies, Barcelona, 1990.

BORRÀS M. L. *Francis Picabia.* Ed. Polígrafa, Barcelona, 1985.

BORRÀS M. L. *Amèlia Riera.* Àmbit, Barcelona, 1990.

BOSCH G. *Museu Municipal de Tossa. Secció d'Art Modern.* Tossa de Mar, 1986.

BOSCH. *El año artístico.* Barcelona (Collection).

BRIHUEGA J. *Las vanguardias artísticas en España. 1909-1936.* Ed. Istmo, Madrid, 1981.

BRIHUEGA J. *La vanguardia y la República.* Ed. Cátedra, S.A., Madrid, 1982.

CADENA J. M. *Jordi Curós.* Àmbit, Barcelona, 1987.

CALLICÓ F. *L'art i la revolució social. Retrats,* Barcelona, 1936.

CALVO SERRALLER F. *El arte visto por los artistas. La vanguardia española analizada por sus protagonistas.* Taurus, Madrid, 1987.

CALVO SERRALLER F. (coordinator) *Doce artistas de vanguardia en el Museo del Prado.* Fundación Amigos del Museo del Prado/Mondadori, Madrid, 1990.

CAPDEVILA F. *Bibliografia de Mn. Manuel Trens i Ribas.* Museu de Vilafranca, Vilafranca del Penedès, 1984.

CAPMANY R DE. *Algunes consideracions eventuals sobre la pintura.* Barcelona, 1950.

CARBONELL J. A. *Francesc Gimeno.* Diccionari Ràfols, Edicions Catalanes, Barcelona, 1987.

CARLES D. *Memorias de un pintor (1912-1930).* Ed. Barna, Barcelona 1944.

CASADO ALCALDE E. *Pintores de la Academia de Roma. Primera promoción.* Lunwerg, Madrid, 1990.

CASAS R., RUSIÑOL S., UTRILLO M. *Viatge a París.* Preface by Francesc Fontbona. Ed. de la Magrana, Barcelona, 1980.

CASELLAS R. *Etapes estètiques.* Vols. I-II, Barcelona, 1916.

CASTELLANOS J. *Raimon Casellas i el Modernisme.* 2 vols., Barcelona, 1983.

CASTELLS PEIG A. *L'art sabadellenc.* Ed. Riutort, Sabadell, 1961.

CASTILLO A. DEL, [CIRICI A.]. *José María Sert.* Barcelona, 1947.

CASTILLO M. *Junceda il·lustrador.* Ayuntamiento de Barcelona, Barcelona, 1990.

CATALUÑA. Tome II. Fundación Juan March, Madrid-Barcelona, 1978.

CELA C. J. *Carlos Mensa. Crónica de una realidad tangente.* Ed. Rayuela, Madrid, 1975.

CERDÀ M. A. *Els pre-rafaelites a Catalunya.* Ed. Curial, Barcelona, 1981.

CHAMORRO P. *Conversaciones con Cuixart.* Ed. Rayuela, Madrid, 1975.

CIRICI A. *El arte modernista catalán.* Aymà, Ed. Barcelona, 1951.

CIRICI A. *L'art català contemporani.* Ed. 62, Barcelona, 1970.

CIRICI A. *Viladecans. Un assaig de lectura.* Ed. 62, Barcelona, 1975.

CIRLOT J. E. "La pintura catalana moderna (1850-1936)," *Historia de la pintura en Cataluña.* Ed. Tecnos, Madrid, n.d., pp. 209-311.

CIRLOT J. E. *El mundo del objeto.* PEN, Barcelona, 1953.

CIRLOT J. E. *La pintura surrealista.* Biblioteca Breve, Barcelona, 1955.

CIRLOT J. E. *Del expresionismo a la abstracción.* Biblioteca Breve, Barcelona, 1955.

CIRLOT J. E. *Cubismo y figuración.* Biblioteca Breve, Barcelona, 1957.

CIRLOT J. E. *El Arte Otro.* Biblioteca Breve, Barcelona, 1957.

CIRLOT J. E. *La pintura de Modest Cuixart.* Barcelona-Paris, 1958.

CIRLOT J. E. *Informalismo.* Ed. Omega, Barcelona, 1959.

CIRLOT J. E. *Roman Vallès.* Barcelona, 1960.

CIRLOT J. E. *Significación de la pintura de Tàpies.* Ed. Seix Barral, Barcelona, 1962.

CIRLOT J. E. *La pintura de Montserrat Gudiol.* Ed. Polígrafa, Barcelona, 1972.

CIRLOT L. *La pintura informal en Cataluña, 1951-1970.* Ed. Anthropos, Barcelona, 1983.

CIRLOT L. *El grupo «Dau al Set».* Ed. Cátedra, Madrid, 1986.

CIRLOT L. *Viladecans. Una aproximació a l'últim període.* Barcelona, 1987.

COLL M. *Bibliografia terrassenca.* Terrassa, 1988.

COMBALIA V. *Tàpies.* Ed. Polígrafa, Barcelona, 1984.

COMBALIA V. *El descubrimiento de Miró. Miró y sus críticos, 1918-1929.* Ed. Destino, Barcelona, 1990.

Vè CONGRÉS ESPANYOL D'HISTÒRIA DE L'ART. ACTES. Vol. II, Barcelona, 1984.

CONTRERAS J. DE. *See* LOZOYA MARQUÉS DE.

CORREDOR-MATHEOS J. *Brotat.* Santander, 1965.

CORREDOR-MATHEOS J. *Arranz-Bravo & Bartolozzi.* Ibérico Europea de Ediciones, Madrid, 1977.

CORREDOR-MATHEOS J. *Guinovart, el arte en libertad.* Ed. Polígrafa, Barcelona, 1981.

CORREDOR-MATHEOS. J. *Montserrat Gudiol. Realidad y símbolo.* Barcelona, 1989.

CORTÈS I VIDAL J. *El pintor Juan Serra.* Librería Editorial Argos, Barcelona, 1942.

CORTÈS I VIDAL J. *Francesc Gimeno.* Barcelona, 1949.

CORTÈS I VIDAL J. *Olivé Busquets (1892-1959).* Barcelona, 1967.

CORTÈS I VIDAL J. *Setanta anys de vida artística barcelonina.* Preface by J. M. Garrut. Ed. Selecta, Barcelona, 1980.

LA CRÍTICA DE ARTE EN ESPAÑA. Publicaciones españolas, Madrid, 1967.

CUIXART. Ed. Rayuela (Cuadernos Guadalimar, 11), Madrid, 1979.

DAIX P., ROSSELET J. *Picasso (1900-1906).* Ed. Blume-Nauta, Barcelona, 1967.

DAIX P., ROSSELET J. *El cubismo de Picasso. Catálogo razonado de la obra pintada, 1907-1916.* Ed. Blume, Barcelona, 1979.

DALÍ A. M. *Noves imatges de Salvador Dalí.* E. Columna, Barcelona 1988.

DALÍ S. *Journal d'un génie.* Introduction and notes by Michel Déon. Gallimard, Paris, 1964.

DALÍ S. *Sí.* Ed. Ariel, Barcelona, Caracas, Mexico City, 1977.

DALÍ S., PARINAUD A. *Confesiones inconfesables.* Ed. Bruguera, S.A., Barcelona, 1975.

DALÍ S. *Vida secreta de Salvador Dalí.* DASA Ed., Figueres, 1981.

DALÍ S. *Los cornudos del viejo arte moderno.* Tusquets Ed., Barcelona, 1990.

DICCIONARIO «RÀFOLS» DE ARTISTAS CONTEMPORÁNEOS DE CATALUÑA Y BALEARES. 4 vols. Diccionari Ràfols, Edicions Catalanes, S.A., Barcelona, 1985-1989 (New edition in 7 vols., 1991).

DOMINGO F. *Luis Washington. Una pintura humana.* São Paulo, 1952.

DUPIN J. *Miró.* Flammarion, Paris, 1961.

DURANCAMPS R. *Lacras de la pintura actual.* Barcelona, 1950.

DURANCAMPS R. Ed. Juventud, Barcelona, 1972.

ELIAS F. *Benet Mercader.* Barcelona, 1921.

ELIAS F. *Simó Gómez.* Barcelona, 1923.

ELIAS F. *Enric Monserdà. La seva vida i la seva obra.* Barcelona, 1927.

ELIAS F. *See also* SACS J.

ELÍAS DE MOLINS A. *Diccionario biográfico y bibliográfico de escritores y artistas catalanes del siglo XIX.* 2 vols., Barcelona, 1889-1895.

ENCICLOPEDIA ESPASA. Ed. Espasa-Calpe, Madrid.

FÀBREGAS E. *Josep de Togores. L'obra. L'home. L'època (1893-1970).* Barcelona, 1970.

FERRANDO J. *Arte religioso actual en Cataluña.* Ed. Atlántida, Barcelona, 1952.

FERRATER G. *Sobre pintura.* Barcelona, 1981.

FESTA MODERNISTA DEL CAU FERRAT. TERCER ANY. CERTAMEN LITERARI CELEBRAT A SITGES EL 4 DE NOVEMBRE DE 1894. Barcelona, 1895 (facsimile ed., Ed. Ausa. Sabadell, 1990).

FIGUERAS I BASSOLS J. M. *Sobre el paper ambigu de l'«amateur» a l'art contemporani.* Barcelona, 1985.

FLAQUER S., PAGÈS M. T. *Inventari d'artistes catalans que participaren als Salons de París fins l'any 1914.* Barcelona, 1986.

FOIX J. V. *97 notes sobre ficcions poncianes. La pell de la pell.* Illustrations by Joan Ponç. Ed. de La Magrana, Barcelona, 1977.

FOIX J. V. *Obres completes.* IV: *Sobre literatura i art.* Ed. 62, Barcelona, 1990.

FOLCH I TORRES J. *El pintor Martí i Alsina.* Junta Municipal d'Exposicions, Barcelona, 1920.

FOLCH I TORRES J. *Fortuny.* Ed. Rosa de Reus, Reus, 1962.

FOLGUERA J. *Articles.* Barcelona, 1920.

FONTBONA F. *La crisi del modernisme artístic.* Ed. Curial, Barcelona, 1975.

FONTBONA F. *El paisatgisme a Catalunya.* Ed. Destino, Barcelona, 1979.

FONTBONA F., MIRALLES F. *Anglada-Camarasa.* Ed. Polígrafa, Barcelona, 1981.

FONTBONA F. *Del Neoclassicisme a la Restauració 1808-1888.* Ed. 62 (Història de l'Art Català, vol. VI), Barcelona, 1983.

FONTBONA F., MIRALLES F. *Del Modernisme al Noucentisme 1888-1917.* Ed. 62 (Història de l'Art Català, vol. VII), Barcelona, 1985.

FONTBONA F. *Pietat Fornesa.* Biographical notice by Joaquim Homs. Àmbit, Barcelona, 1987.

FRANCÈS J. *El año artístico.* Madrid (Collection).

FRANCIN F. *Picasso y Horta de Ebro.* Tarragona, 1981.

FUSTER J., PONÇ J. *Exploració de l'ombra.* Barcelona, 1974.

FUSTER M. *La acuarela y sus aplicaciones.* Madrid-Barcelona, 1893.

GALÍ F. *Rollan.* Barcelona, 1977.

GALWEY E. *El que he vist a Can Parés en els darrers quaranta anys.* Sala Parés, Barcelona, 1934.

García Martín M. *Vidrieras de un gran jardín de vidrios*. Preface by A. Cirici. Catalana de Gas i Electricitat, Barcelona, 1981.

García Martín M. *Els vitralls cloisonné de Barcelona*. Barcelona, 1985.

Garriga J. *Joan Vila Cinca. Notícia sobre l'obra i la vida del pintor*. Ed. Juventud, Barcelona, 1975.

Garrut J. M. *Dos siglos de pintura catalana (XIX-XX)*. Ibérico Europea de ediciones, Madrid, 1974.

Gasch S. *L'expansió de l'art català al món*. Barcelona, 1953.

Gasch S. *Escrits d'art i d'avantguarda (1925-1938)*. Ed. del Mall, Barcelona, 1987.

Gavaldà J. V. *La tradició avantguardista catalana. Proses de Gorkiano i Salvat-Papasseit*. Biblioteca Serra d'Or, Barcelona, 1988.

Gaya Nuño J. A. *La pintura española fuera de España (Historia y catálogo)*. Espasa-Calpe, Madrid, 1958.

Gaya Nuño J. A. *Historia de la crítica de arte en España*. Madrid, 1975.

Gent nostra. Edicions de Nou Art Thor, Barcelona (Volumes published: 4: Gimeno; 9: Rusiñol; 17: Dalí; 18: Vayreda; 19: Fortuny; 26: Mir; 47: Opisso; 51: Nonell).

Gimferrer P. *Antoni Tàpies i l'esperit català*. Ed. Polígrafa, Barcelona, 1974.

González C., Martí M. *Pintores españoles en Roma (1850-1900)*. Tusquets, Barcelona, 1987.

González C., Martí M. *Mariano Fortuny Marsal*, 2 vols. Preface by Joan Ainaud. Diccionari Ràfols, Edicions Catalanes, Barcelona, 1989.

Gran enciclopèdia catalana, 17 volums. Barcelona, 1969-1989 (there exists as well a second edition differing in both format and number of volumes).

Grandes dibujantes. (Collection).

Gudiol J. M., Alcolea Gil S., Cirlot J. de. *Historia de la pintura en Cataluña*. Ed. Tecnos, Madrid, n.d.

Guía para el estudio de la pintura. Biblioteca de Ciencias, Artes y Oficios, Barcelona, 1861.

Història gràfica de Catalunya dia a dia. Ed. 62, Barcelona, 1979 *et sq*.

Homenaje a Eugenio d'Ors. Academia del Faro de San Cristóbal, Madrid, 1968.

Homenatge de Catalunya a Alexandre Cirici (1914-1983). Barcelona, 1984 (Contains a biographical notice).

Homenatge de Catalunya a Picasso. Fundació Picasso-Reventós, Barcelona, 1982.

Iglésies J. *Baldomer Galofre Ximenis*. Edicions Rosa de Reus, Reus, 1953.

Infiesta J. M. *¿Artistas o filisteos? Manifiesto contra el arte académico actual*. Barcelona, 1976.

Infiesta J. M. *Josep Llimona i Joan Llimona. Vida i obra*. Barcelona, 1977.

Jacob M. *Saint Matorel*. D. H. Kahnweiler, Paris, 1910.

Jardí E. *Nonell i altres assaigs*. Ed. Selecta, Barcelona, 1958.

Jardí E. *Eugeni d'Ors. Vida i obra*. Ed. Aymà, Barcelona, 1967 (2nd ed. 1991).

Jardí E. et al. *L'art català contemporani*. Ed. Proa, Barcelona, 1972.

Jardí E. *Història de Els Quatre Gats*. Ed. Aedos, Barcelona, 1972.

Jardí E. *Les arts plàstiques a Catalunya en el darrer segle*. Raixa, Palma de Mallorca, 1973.

Jardí E. *Torres Garcia*. Ed. Polígrafa, Barcelona, 1973.

Jardí E. *Història del Cercle Artístic de Sant Lluc*. Barcelona, 1976.

Jardí E. *Jaume Mercadé. Pintor de una tierra*. Ed. Polígrafa, Barcelona, 1977.

Jardí E. *Las Bellas Artes*. Diputación Provincial de Barcelona, Barcelona, 1977.

Jardí E. *El Noucentisme*. Barcelona, 1980.

Jardí E. *El cartellisme a Catalunya*. Ed. Destino, Barcelona, 1983.

Jardí E. *Nonell*. Ed. Polígrafa, Barcelona, 1984.

Jardí E. *Nou converses amb Jordi Mercadé*. Barcelona, 1985.

Jardí E. *Gimeno*. Àmbit, Barcelona, 1985.

Jardí E., Calsina R. *Calsina*. Barcelona, 1990.

Jordà J. M. *Ramon Casas, pintor*. Barcelona, 1931.

Julian I. *Les avantguardes pictòriques a Catalunya al segle XX*. Preface by Ricard Salvat. Els llibres de la Frontera, Sant Cugat del Vallès, 1986.

Junoy J. M. *Arte y artistas*. Barcelona, 1912.

Junoy J. M. *L'actualitat artística. 1930-1931*. Barcelona, 1931.

Labarta F. *Para comprender la pintura*. Dalmau, Barcelona, 1944.

Llimona J. *De lo essencial i de lo accidental en l'Art. Discurs llegit l'1 de juliol de 1917*. Acadèmia Provincial de Belles Arts, Barcelona, 1917.

Llimona J. *Joan Llimona (1860-1926): El do de Déu. Recull d'articles i escrits diversos*. Ed. Políglota, Barcelona, 1930.

Llongueras J. (Chiron). *Ínfimes cròniques d'alta civilitat*. Terrassa, 1911.

López Jiménez J. *See* Pantorba B. de.

Lozoya Marqués de (J. de Contreras). *Santiago Padrós. Vida y obra (1918-1971)*. Editora Nacional, Madrid, 1972.

Maestros actuales de la pintura y escultura catalanas. Ed. La Gran Enciclopedia Vasca – Edicions Catalanes. Bilbao-Barcelona. Series of monographs begun in 1974. More than 70 works currently in progress.

Maestros contemporáneos del dibujo y la pintura. Cuadernos de arte. Ibérico Europea de Ediciones, Madrid, 1970 *et sq.* (Collection).

Maestros de la pintura española contemporánea. A. Aguado, Ed. Madrid, 1952 *et sq.* (Collection).

Maestros del arte de los siglos XIX y XX. Barcelona. Diccionari Ràfols, Edicions Catalanes. Publication in progress.

Manent A. *Josep Carner i el noucentisme. Vida, obra i llegenda.* Ed. 62, Barcelona, 1969.

Manent M. *Notícies d'art.* Ed. 62, Barcelona, 1981.

Manzano R., Jardí E., Trens J. *Josep Amat o el impresionismo catalán.* Barcelona, 1986.

Manzano R. *Pere Ysern Alié 1875-1946.* Preface by Francesc Fontbona. Diccionari Ràfols, Edicions Catalanes, Barcelona, 1990.

Maragall J. A. *Història de la Sala Parés.* Preface by J. Ainaud. Ed. Selecta, Barcelona, 1975.

Marès F. *La enseñanza artística en Barcelona.* Discussion with F. Labarta, Barcelona, 1954.

Marès F. *Dos siglos de enseñanza artística en el Principado.* Reial Acadèmia de Belles Arts de Sant Jordi, Barcelona, 1964.

Marquina R. *Ricardo Canals.* Monografías de Arte, Madrid.

Ramon Martí Alsina. Almanac de La Revista, Barcelona, 1919.

Martinell C. *La Escuela de la Lonja en la vida artística barcelonesa.* Barcelona, 1951.

Masriera J. *Círculo artístico de Barcelona. Sesión necrológica dedicada a D. Claudio Lorenzale.* Barcelona, 1889-1890.

Masriera J. *Discurso necrológico del eminente artista D. José Luis Pellicer.* Academia Provincial de Bellas Artes, Barcelona, 1903.

Mates J. *La jove pintura local.* Sabadell, 1927.

Mates J. *Vila-Puig.* Barcelona, 1934.

Mates J. *El pintor Gimeno.* Barcelona, 1935 (2nd ed. Sabadell, 1988, with an essay by F. Miralles, *Aproximació a Joan Mates*).

McCully M. *Els Quatre Gats. Art in Barcelona around 1900.* The Art Museum, Princeton University, Princeton, 1978.

Mendoza C., Mendoza E. *Barcelona modernista.* Ed. Planeta, Barcelona, 1989.

Merli J. *33 pintors catalans.* Comissariat de Propaganda de la Generalitat de Catalunya, Barcelona, 1937 (2nd ed., 1976).

Mialet P. *Jaume Mercadé, pintor i orfebre.* Estudis vallencs, Valls, 1970.

Miquel Farré, Pintor. IMM. Barcelona, 1990.

Mirabent Soler F. de P. *Cómo pintaba las flores y las frutas mi padre, el pintor don José Mirabent Gatell (1831-1899).* With preliminary notes by R. Díez Campañà. (Original of 45 leaves conserved in the Biblioteca dels Museus d'Art de Barcelona.)

Miralles F. *Pere Torné Esquius.* Barcelona 1987.

Miralles F. *L'època de les avantguardes 1917-1970.* Ed. 62 (Història de l'Art Català, vol. VIII), Barcelona, 1983.

Miró J. *Ceci est la couleur de mes rêves. Entretiens avec Georges Raillard.* Seuil, Paris, 1977.

Miró J. *Epistolari català.* Edition and notes by J. Ainaud (Manuscript).

Molas J., Marín Medina J., Puig A. *Dau al set.* Ed. Rayuela (Cuadernos Guadalimar, 7), Madrid, 1978.

Molas J. *La literatura catalana d'avantguarda. 1916-1938.* Anthology selection, edition and accompanying study by Molas. Antoni Bosch, Ed., Barcelona, 1983.

Monografías de artistas españoles contemporáneos (Collection).

Mora Piris P. *Josep Cusachs.* Introduction by Daniel Giralt-Miracle. Diccionari Ràfols, Edicions Catalanes, Barcelona, 1988.

Moreno S. *El pintor Pelegrín Clavé.* Instituto de Investigaciones Estéticas, Mexico City, 1966.

Moreno S. *El escultor Manuel Vilar.* Instituto de Investigaciones Estéticas, Mexico City, 1969.

Moreno S. *El pintor Antonio Fabrés.* Instituto de Investigaciones Estéticas, Mexico City, 1981.

Moreno Galván J. M. *La última vanguardia. Pintura Española.* Magius, Madrid, 1969.

Moreno y Rivera T. *Nicolau Raurich i Pietri: estudio biográfico-crítico y catálogo razonado de su producción pictórica.* Universitat de Barcelona. Thesis on 20 microfilms.

Nadal Gaya J. M. *Pintura y pintores leridanos del siglo XX.* Instituto de Estudios llerdenses, Lleida, 1968.

Neuvillate A. de. *Francisco Goitia precursor de la escuela mexicana.* Universidad Nacional Autónoma de México, 1964.

L'Obra d'Isidre Nonell. La Revista, Barcelona, 1917.

Omer M. *Universo y magia de Joan Ponç.* Ed. Polígrafa, Barcelona, 1972.

Opisso A. *Arte y artistas catalanes.* La Vanguardia, Barcelona, 1900 (reprint: Banca Mas Sardà, Barcelona, 1977).

Ors E. d' *Mis salones. Itinerario del arte moderno en España.* M. Aguilar Ed., Madrid.

Ors E. d' *Cincuenta años de pintura catalana.* Barcelona, 1925 (Manuscript).

Ors E. d' *La Ben Plantada. Galeria de Noucentistes.* Preface by Enric Jardí. Ed. Selecta, Barcelona, 1976.

Ors E. d' *Nuevo Glosario.* vol. I *(1920-1926);* vol. II *(1927-1933);* vol. III *(1934-1943).* M. Aguilar Ed., Madrid, 1947-1949.

ORS E. D' *Novísimo Glosario (1944-1945)*. M. Aguilar Ed., Madrid, 1946.

ORS E. D' *Glosari (selecció)*. Ed. 62, Barcelona, 1982.

OSSORIO Y BERNARD M. *Galería biográfica de artistas españoles del siglo XIX*. Imprenta de Moreu y Rojas, Madrid, 1883-1884.

PALAU I FABRE J. *Picasso vivent (1881-1907)*. Ed. Polígrafa, Barcelona, 1980.

PALAU I FABRE J. *Nous quaderns de l'Alquimista*. Ed. del Mall, Barcelona, 1983.

PALAU I FABRE J. *Picasso cubista*. Ed. Polígrafa, Barcelona, 1990.

PANTORBA B. DE (JOSÉ LÓPEZ JIMÉNEZ). *Eliseo Meifrén, ensayo biográfico y crítico*. Delta, Barcelona, 1942.

PANTORBA B. DE (JOSÉ LÓPEZ JIMÉNEZ). *Historia y crítica de las Exposiciones Nacionales de Bellas Artes celebradas en España*. Ed. Alcor, Madrid, 1948.

PANYELLA V. *Epistolari del Cau Ferrat. 1889-1930*. Preface by R. Planes. Grup d'estudis sitgetans, Sitges, 1981.

PARCERISAS P. *Grau-Garriga*. Ed. Polígrafa, Barcelona, 1987.

PARCERISAS P. *Aurèlia Muñoz*. Testimonis d'Art, Barcelona, 1990.

PELLICER J. L. *Joseph Ll. Pellicer*. Lectura popular n.º 206, pp. 417-448.

PELLICER J. L. *Notas y dibujos*. Vols. I-II. La Vanguardia, Barcelona.

PENROSE R. *Tàpies*. Ed. Polígrafa, Barcelona, 1977.

PENROSE R. *80 años de surrealismo. 1900-1981*. Ed. Polígrafa, Barcelona, 1981.

PÉREZ ROJAS J. *Art déco en España*. Ed. Cátedra, Madrid, 1990.

PIERRE J., CORREDOR-MATHEOS J. *Céramiques de Miró et Artigas*. Maeght Ed., Paris, 1974.

LA PINTURA INFORMALISTA EN ESPAÑA A TRAVÉS DE LOS CRÍTICOS. Dirección General de Relaciones Culturales, Madrid, 1961.

PLA I CASADEVALL J. *Retrats de passaport*. Ed. Destino (Obra Completa, 17), Barcelona, 1970.

PLA I CASADEVALL J. *Homenots. 4.ª sèrie*. Ed. Destino (Obra Completa de Josep Pla, 29), Barcelona, 1975.

PLA I PALLEJÀ J. *Els gravats de Xavier Nogués*. Ed. de la Rosa Vera, Barcelona, 1960.

PLANAS M. R. *Enric-Cristòfol Ricart, gravador del noucentisme*. Biblioteca de Catalunya, Barcelona, 1988.

PLANES R. *El Modernisme a Sitges*. Ed. Selecta, Barcelona, 1969.

PLANES R. *Santiago Rusiñol per ell mateix*. Under the direction of Planes. Ed. 62 (Antologia Catalana), Barcelona, 1971.

PORCEL B. *La palabra del arte*. Madrid, 1976.

PUIG A. *El pensament artístic actual*. Quaderns de Cultura, Ed. Bruguera, Barcelona, 1967.

PUIG PERUCHO B. *La pintura de paisaje*. Suc. de E. Meseguer, Barcelona, 1971 (3rd ed.).

PUJOLS F. *Recull d'articles de crítica artística*. La Revista, Barcelona, 1921.

PUJOLS F. *Articles*. Ed. dels Quaderns Crema, Barcelona, 1984.

[RÀFOLS J. F.]. *Catálogo de pintura y dibujo del «Cau Ferrat» (Fundación Rusiñol). Sitges*. Barcelona, 1942.

RÀFOLS J. F. *Modernismo y modernistas*. Ed. Destino, Barcelona, 1949 (Catalan transl. 1982).

RÀFOLS J. F. *El arte romántico en España*. Ed. Juventud, Barcelona, 1954.

RÀFOLS J. F. *Ramon Casas, pintor*. Ed. Omega, Barcelona, n.d.

RÀFOLS J. F. *Ramon Casas, dibujante*. Ed. Omega, Barcelona, n.d.

RÀFOLS J. F. *E. C. Ricart*. El cep i la nansa. Ed. Vilanova i la Geltrú, 1981.

RÀFOLS CASAMADA A. *L'escorça dels dies. Fulls de dietari. 1975-1977*. Laertes, Barcelona 1984.

RECUERDO DE LA INAUGURACIÓN DEL MONUMENTO A PEPITA TEIXIDOR. Barcelona, 1921.

RENART J. *Diari 1918-1961*. Ed. Destino, Barcelona, 1975.

RENART J. *Apunts de Centelles*. Text and drawings by Renart. Sabadell, 1990.

RIBA C. *Cartes de Carles Riba. I: 1910-1938. Recollides i anotades per Carles-Jordi Guardiola*. Institut d'Estudis Catalans, Barcelona, 1989.

RIBÉ M. C. *«La Revista» (1915-1936). La seva estructura. El seu contingut*. Ed. Barcino, Barcelona, 1983.

RODRÍGUEZ AGUILERA C. *J. M. García Llort*. Ateneo de Madrid, Madrid, 1963.

RODRÍGUEZ AGUILERA C. *Guinovart*. Ministerio de Educación y Ciencia (Artistas Españoles Contemporáneos), Madrid, 1971.

RODRÍGUEZ AGUILERA C. *Coll Bardolet*. Àmbit, Barcelona, 1980.

RODRÍGUEZ AGUILERA C. *Arte moderno en Cataluña. Examen de qué cosa sea arte y qué cosa modernidad*. Preface by Pere Gimferrer. Ed. Planeta, Barcelona, 1986.

RODRÍGUEZ CODOLÁ M. *Un pintor catalán del siglo pasado. José Masriera*. Barcelona, 1934.

ROMERO L. *Tharrats*. Publicaciones La isla de los ratones, Santander, 1961.

RUBIN W. *Picasso et Braque. L'invention du cubisme*. Flammarion, Paris, 1990.

RUIZ Y PABLO A. *Historia de la Real Junta Particular de Comercio de Barcelona (1758 a 1847)*. Cambra de Comerç i Navegació, Barcelona, 1919.

RUSIÑOL S. *Desde el molino*. Barcelona, 1894.

RUSIÑOL S. *Impresiones de arte*. Barcelona, 1897.

SABARTÉS J. *Picasso. Retratos y recuerdos*. A. Aguado, Madrid, 1953.

SACS J. (FELIU ELIAS). *La pintura francesa moderna fins al cubisme*. Preface by J. Folguera. La Revista, Barcelona, 1917.

SACS J. (FELIU ELIAS). *Joan Brull (1863-1912). Evocació d'un pintor barceloní del temps del modernisme*. Biblioteca Galeries Dalmau, Barcelona, 1926.

SACS J. (FELIU ELIAS). *Joan Colom. Artista Contemporani*. Barcelona, 1929.

SALRACH J. M. *Història de Catalunya*. Director of the edition D. Salvat Editores, S.A. Vols. V-VI, Barcelona, 1979.

SÁNCHEZ CAMARGO M. "Historia de la Academia Breve de Crítica de Arte," *Homenaje a Eugenio d'Ors*. Madrid, 1963.

SANOUILLET M. *Francis Picabia et 391*. 2 vols. Le Terrain Vague, Paris, 1960 and 1966.

SANTOS TORROELLA R. *Del románico al pop art*. EDHASA, Barcelona, 1965.

SANTOS TORROELLA R. *Manuel Capdevila y la «generación prohibida»*. Barcelona, 1972.

SANTOS TORROELLA R. *Francisco Miralles (1848-1901)*. Editorial RM, Barcelona, 1974.

SANTOS TORROELLA R. *La miel es más dulce que la sangre. Las épocas lorquiana y freudiana de Salvador Dalí*. Ed. Seix Barral, Barcelona, 1984.

SANTOS TORROELLA R. *Salvador Dalí corresponsal de J. V. Foix. 1932-1936*. Ed. Mediterrània, Barcelona, 1986.

SANTOS TORROELLA R. *Ramon Pichot*. Ed. Àmbit, Barcelona, 1986.

SAURET T. *El siglo XIX en la pintura malagueña*. Universidad de Málaga, Málaga, 1987.

SEGHERS P. *Clavé*. Ed. Polígrafa, Barcelona, 1972.

SELECCIÓN DE ARTE ACTUAL. 2 vols, Barcelona.

SEMPRONIO. *See* ARTÍS A.A.

SERRA F. *L'aventura de l'art contemporani (l'artista i la seva època)*. Ed. Selecta, Barcelona, 1978.

SERRA DIMAS F. *Nuestros artistas*. Edimar, Barcelona, 1954.

SERRA P. A. *Miró y Mallorca*. Ed. Polígrafa, Barcelona, 1984.

SIMA M. *24 perfiles de artistas*. Enlarged by F. P. Verrié Ed. Vergara, Barcelona, 1961.

SISQUELLA A. *Decorativismo y realismo. (Deshumanización y humanización de la pintura moderna)*. Edimar, Barcelona, 1954.

SOCIAS PALAU J. *Canals*. Ed. Espasa Calpe, Barcelona, 1976.

SOCIAS PALAU J. "Pintura," *Modernisme a Catalunya*. Barcelona, 1982, pp. 7-154.

SOCIAS PALAU J. *Puigdengolas*. Ed. Marzo, Barcelona, 1988.

SOLDEVILA C. *Barcelona vista pels seus artistes*. Ed. Aedos, Barcelona, 1957.

SOLDEVILA C. *Records i opinions de Pere Ynglada recollits per –*. Barcelona, 1959.

SUÀREZ A. *Pintura i crítica. Un estudi sobre Rafael Benet*. Publicaciones de la Universidad de Barcelona, Barcelona, 1980.

SUCRE J. M. DE. *Memorias. I. Del Romanticismo al Modernismo; II: Los primeros pasos del 1900*. Ed. Barna, S.A., Barcelona, 1963.

ANTONI TÀPIES. Ed. Rayuela (Cuadernos Guadalimar, 6), Madrid, 1978.

TÀPIES A. *La pràctica de l'art*. Ariel, Barcelona [1970].

TÀPIES A. *L'art contra l'estètica*. Ariel, Barcelona, 1974.

TÀPIES A. *Memòria personal*. Ed. Crítica, Barcelona, 1977.

TÀPIES A. *La realitat com a art*. Ed. Laertes, Barcelona, 1982.

TÀPIES A. *Per un art modern i progressista*. Empúries, Barcelona, 1985.

TEIXIDOR J. *Entre les Lletres i les Arts*. Barcelona, 1957.

TEIXIDOR J. *Els Antics*. Barcelona, 1968.

TEIXIDOR J. *Tot apuntat. 1965-1975*. Barcelona, 1981.

TEIXIDOR J. *Els anys i els llocs*. Barcelona, 1985.

TEIXIDOR J. *Apunts encara. 1983-1985*. Barcelona, 1986.

TEIXIDOR J. *Més apunts. 1986-1989*. Barcelona, 1990.

THARRATS J. J. *Antoni Tàpies o el Dau Modern de Versalles*. Dau al Set, Barcelona, 1950.

THARRATS J. J. *Cent anys de pintura a Cadaqués*. Ediciones del Cotal, S.A., Badalona, 1981.

TORNÉ ESQUIUS P. *Els dolços indrets de Catalunya*. Vilanova i la Geltrú, 1910.

TORRAS I BAGES J. *De la fruïció artística*. Cercle Artístic de Sant Lluc, Barcelona, 1894.

TORRES-GARCIA J. *Universalismo constructivo*. Ed. Poseidón, Buenos Aires, 1944.

TORRES-GARCIA J. *Escrits sobre art*. Ed. 62, Barcelona, 1980.

TORRES-GARCIA J. *Historia de mi vida*. Ed. Paidós Ibérica, Barcelona, 1990 (1st ed., Montevideo, 1939).

TRENC BALLESTER E. *Les arts gràfiques de l'època modernista a Barcelona*. Barcelona, 1977.

UN SEGLE DE VIDA CATALANA 1814-1930. 2 vols, Ed. Alcides, Barcelona, 1961.

URGELL M. *Catalunya*. Barcelona, 1905.

URGELL M. *El murciélago. Memorias de una Patum*. Barcelona, 1919.

UTRILLO M. *Història anecdòtica del Cau Ferrat*. Preface by Francesc Fontbona. Grup d'Estudis sitgetans (Quaderns, 18), Sitges, 1989.

VALLCORBA PLANA J. *Josep Maria Junoy. Obra poètica*. Study and edition by Vallcorba Plana Ed. dels Quaderns Crema, Barcelona, 1984.

VALLÈS E. *La cultura contemporània a Catalunya (1888-1931)*. Barcelona, 1977.

VALLÈS E. *Història gràfica de la Catalunya contemporània*. Ed. 62, Vols. I-III, Barcelona, 1974-1976.

VALLÈS E. *Història gràfica de la Catalunya autònoma*. Ed. 62, Vols. I-II, Barcelona, 1977-1978.

VALLÈS E. *Història gràfica de Catalunya sota el règim franquista*. Ed. 62, Barcelona, 1980.

VALLÈS J. *Tàpies empremta (art-vida)*. Ed. Robrenyo. Barcelona, 1983 (2nd ed.).

VALVERDE J. M. *Cartas a un cura escéptico en materia de arte moderno*. Biblioteca Breve, Barcelona, 1959.

VENTALLÓ J. *Notes biogràfiques de l'eminent artista terrassenc Francisco Torras Armengol...* Ayuntamiento de Terrassa, Terrassa, 1916.

VERGÉS G. *El pintor tortosí Antoni Casanova (1847-1896)*. Tortosa, 1983.

VERRIÉ F. P. *El pintor Pidelaserra, ensayo de biografía crítica*. Barcelona, 1947.

VIDAL M. *Teoria i crítica del Noucentisme: Joaquim Folch i Torres*. Institut d'Estudis Catalans, Barcelona, 1991.

VIDAL P. *Els singulars anecdòtics*. J. Horta Ed., Barcelona, 1920.

VIDAL I SORDÉ J. *Antoni Samarra i Tuges, l'home i l'artista (1886-1914)*. Portaveu, Ponts, 1982.

VIGÓ A. *Joaquim Espalter i Rull (en el centenari de la seva mort)*. Grup d'Estudis sitgetans (Quaderns, 10), Sitges, 1980.

VILA ARRUFAT. Fundació Amics de les Lletres de Sabadell (Quadern), Sabadell, 1987.

VILA CASAS J. *Escrits de Joan Vila Casas*. Barcelona, 1954.

VILA CASAS J. *Doble blanc*. Barcelona, 1960.

VILA CASAS J. *Matèria definitiva*. Barcelona, 1961.

VILA CASAS J. *Operació viaducte*. Barcelona, 1962.

VILA CASAS J. *Cartes a un pintor*. L'Hospitalet, 1964.

VILA CASAS J. *Jourdain 65*. Barcelona, 1965.

VILA CASAS J. *Nnoba fygurassió*. Sant Cugat del Vallès, 1965.

VILA CASAS J. *Aiguafort del XII*. Barcelona, 1966.

VILA CASAS J. *Jourdain 65*. Barcelona, 1966.

VILA-GRAU. Cuadernos Guadalimar, 15. Madrid, 1978.

VILA-GRAU J., RODON F. *Els vitrallers de la Barcelona modernista*. Ed. Polígrafa, Barcelona, 1982.

VILAR P. *Història de Catalunya*. Vols. V to VIII. Directed by Vilar. Ed. 62, Barcelona, 1987-1990.

VOLTES P. *Abelló*. Publicaciones Reunidas, Badalona, 1974.

YXART J. *Fortuny. Noticia biográfica crítica*. Biblioteca «Arte y Letras», Barcelona, 1881.

PERIODICAL PUBLICATIONS

A ESTUDIOS PRO ARTE. Barcelona, 1975-1978.

D'ACÍ I D'ALLÀ. MAGAZINE CATALÀ. Llibreria Catalònia, Barcelona, 1918-1936.

ÁLBUM SALÓN. Barcelona, 1897-1907.

ALGOL. Barcelona, 1950.

ALMANAC DE LA REVISTA. Barcelona, 1919.

L'AMIC DE LES ARTS. Sitges, 1926-1929.

ANALES Y BOLETÍN DE LOS MUSEOS DE ARTE DE BARCELONA. Vols. I-VI, Barcelona, 1941-1948.

ARC VOLTAIC. Barcelona, 1918.

ARCHIVO ESPAÑOL DE ARTE. Madrid, 1925 *et sq.*

ARIEL. REVISTA DE LES ARTS. Barcelona, 1946-1951.

ART. Barcelona, 1933-1936.

D'ART. Departamento de Historia del Arte de la Universidad de Barcelona, 1972 *et sq.*

ART BIBLIOGRAPHICS MODERN. Oxford.

ART. GUIA MENSUAL DE LES ARTS. Barcelona, 1987 *et sq.*

ARTE. REVISTA MENSUAL DE LAS ARTES. Barcelona, 1989 *et sq.*

ARTE ESPAÑOL. Sociedad Española de Amigos del Arte, Madrid.

ARTEGUÍA. REVISTA MENSUAL DE ARTE. Madrid, 1973 *et sq.*

ÀRTICS. Barcelona, 1985-1990.

L'ARTPORDÀ. Barcelona, 1988 *et sq.*

ARTS. REVISTA DEL CERCLE DE BELLES ARTS. Lleida, 1990.

ARTUAL. Barcelona.

BALUART. Sitges.

BATIK. Barcelona, 1973 *et sq.*

BUTLLETÍ DE LA REIAL ACADÈMIA CATALANA DE BELLES ARTS DE SANT JORDI. Barcelona, 1986 *et sq.*

BUTLLETÍ DEL CENTRE DE LECTURA DE REUS. Reus.

CAHIERS D'ART. Paris.

CATALUNYA. Barcelona, 1903-1905.

CATALUNYA ARTÍSTICA. Barcelona, 1900-1903.

CULTURA. Girona, 1914 (*Cultura. Una revista gironina de l'any 1914. Edició facsímil.* Ed. del Cotal. Barcelona, 1979).

CULTURA. BUTLLETÍ DEL DEPARTAMENT DE CULTURA DE LA GENERALITAT DE CATALUNYA. Barcelona, 1983 *et sq.*

DAU AL SET. Barcelona, September 1948 - December 1956.

EL DIA. Terrassa.

DIARI D'ART. Sant Cugat del Vallès, 1986.

DIARIO DE BARCELONA. Barcelona.

EL ECO DE SITGES. Sitges.

UN ENEMIC DEL POBLE. FULLA DE SUBVERSIÓ ESPIRITUAL. Barcelona, 1917-1919. (Facsimile: Artis Ed., Barcelona, 1976.)

ESPAIS. PAPERS D'ART. Girona.

EX-LIBRIS. QUADERNS D'INVESTIGACIÓ EXLIBRÍSTICA. Barcelona, 1989 *et sq.*

FORMA. Barcelona, 1904-1907.

FUTURISME. REVISTA CATALANA. Barcelona, 1907.

GAL ART. REVISTA DE ARTE. Barcelona, 1988 *et sq.*

GASETA DE LES ARTS. Barcelona.

GAZETA DEL ARTE. EXPOSICIONES Y SUBASTAS. Madrid, 1973 *et sq.*

GOYA. REVISTA DE ARTE. Madrid, 1954 *et sq.*

GUADALIMAR. REVISTA DE ARTE. Madrid, 1975 *et sq.*

EL GUÍA. MENSUAL DE LA CULTURA VISUAL. Barcelona, 1988 *et sq.*

HÈLIX. Vilafranca del Penedès, 1929-1930.

HISPANIA. Barcelona, 1899-1903.

L'HOME INVISIBLE. Barcelona, 1989 *et sq.*

IL·LUSTRACIÓ CATALANA. Barcelona, 1880-1917.

LA ILUSTRACIÓN ARTÍSTICA. Barcelona, 1882-1916.

INFORMATIU DE LES ARTS PLÀSTIQUES. Generalitat de Catalunya, Barcelona, 1988 *et sq.*

L'INSTANT. Paris and Barcelona, 1918-1919.

JOVENTUT. Barcelona, 1900-1906.

LÁPIZ. Madrid, 1982 *et sq.*

LA LLUMANERA DE NOVA YORK. New York, 1874-1881.

LA MÀ TRENCADA. Edicions Joan Merli. Barcelona, 6 November 1924 - 31 January 1925. (Facsimile: Leteradura [Ready Mades coll.], Barcelona, 1977.)

LUZ. Barcelona, 1897-1898.

MARTE. Barcelona.

EL MATÍ. Barcelona, 24 May 1929 - 19 July 1936.

METRÒNOM. ART CONTEMPORANI. Barcelona, 1984 *et sq.*

MISCELLANEA BARCINONENSIA. I-XLVIII. Barcelona, 1962-1977.

MONITOR. Sitges.

MUSEUM. REVISTA DE ARTE ESPAÑOL ANTIGUO Y MODERNO Y DE LA VIDA ARTÍSTICA. Barcelona, 1911-1927.

NAHUYA.

NEGRE +... REVISTA D'ART I POESIA. Ed. del Cotal, Barcelona, 1983 *et sq.*

LA NOVA REVISTA. Barcelona, 1927-1929.

PAPELES DE SON ARMADANS. Palma de Mallorca, 1956-1979.

PÈL & PLOMA. Barcelona, 1899-1903. (Facsimile: Leteradura, Barcelona, 1977.)

LA PUBLICIDAD. Barcelona.

LA PUBLICITAT. Barcelona.

QUADERNS D'ESTUDI. Barcelona.

QUATRE GATS. Barcelona, 1899.

QÜERN. Olot, 1986-1988.

QÜESTIONS D'ART. LA REVISTA CATALANA D'ART ACTUAL. Barcelona, 1966 *et sq.*

REIAL ACADÈMIA CATALANA DE BELLES ARTS DE SANT JORDI. BUTLLETÍ. Barcelona, 1986 *et sq.*

LA REVISTA. Barcelona, 1914 *et sq.*

REVISTA DE CATALUNYA. Barcelona.

REVISTA DE GERONA. Girona, 1955 *et sq.* (From 1976: REVISTA DE GIRONA.)

REVISTA DE LLEIDA. Lleida.

SAN JORGE. Diputación de Barcelona. Barcelona.

SERRA D'OR. Montserrat-Barcelona, 1955 *et sq.*

TASCÓ. Escola Taller d'Art. Diputación de Tarragona. Reus, 1979 *et sq.*

IL TIBERIO (Manuscript).

LA VANGUARDIA. Barcelona.

VELL I NOU. Barcelona, 1915-1922.

LA VEU DE CATALUNYA. Barcelona.

VITRINA. Olot, 1985 *et sq.*

CATALOGUES AND GUIDES

GENERAL

A Catálogos del Centre d'Art Alexandre Cirici. L'Hospitalet de Llobregat.

ACADEMIA BREVE DE CRÍTICA DE ARTE. ÚLTIMA EXPOSICIÓN. WINTER 1955.

HOMENAJE A EUGENIO D'ORS. Madrid, 1955.

ACTIVIDADES ARTÍSTICAS. Sala Gaspar. Barcelona, 1946.

ANTOLOGÍA DE LA I BIENAL HISPANOAMERICANA DE ARTE. Barcelona, 1952.

ART CATALÀ CONTEMPORANI (1970-1985). Fons d'Art de Xarxa Cultural, Barcelona, 1985.

ART CONTEMPORANI. CATALUNYA NORD. Xarxa Cultural, Perpignan, 1989.

L'ART ESPANYOL EN LA COL·LECCIÓ DE LA FUNDACIÓ CAIXA DE PENSIONS. Barcelona, 1987.

121 ARTISTAS CATALANES DE 1937. Madrid, 1980.

ARTISTAS ESPAÑOLES CONTEMPORÁNEOS. Ministerio de Educación y Ciencia, Madrid (Series of catalogues.)

ARTISTES GIRONINS. 1800-1900. Casa de la Cultura, Girona, 1974.

ELS AUTORETRATS DEL MUSEU D'ART MODERN. Ayuntamiento de Barcelona, Barcelona, 1983.

II BIENAL HISPANOAMERICANA DE ARTE. CATÁLOGO DE LA MUESTRA ESPAÑOLA. Havana, 1954.

II BIENAL HISPANOAMERICANA DE ARTE. CATÁLOGO GENERAL. Havana, 1954.

III BIENAL HISPANOAMERICANA DE ARTE. CATÁLOGO OFICIAL. Barcelona, 1955-1956.

BIENAL INTERNACIONAL DE PINTURA. PREMIO F. ESTRADA SALADICH. Barcelona, 1967.

I BIENAL INTERNACIONAL S.E.U. DE ARTE UNIVERSITARIO DE IBIZA. Barcelona, 1965.

BIENNAL D'ART. Valls, 1990.

BIENNAL D'ART FUTBOL CLUB BARCELONA. Barcelona (1985 and 1987).

BIENNAL DE JOVE PINTURA CONTEMPORÀNIA. Fundació Caixa de Barcelona, Barcelona (1975 et sq.).

CATÀLEG DE L'EXPOSICIÓ DE PINTURA DEL CONCURS PLANDIURA 1922-1923. Galeries Laietanes, Barcelona, 1923.

CATÀLEG DE PINTURA. SEGLES XIX I XX. FONS DEL MUSEU D'ART MODERN. 2 vols, Ayuntamiento de Barcelona, Barcelona, 1987.

CATÁLOGO DE LA EXPOSICIÓN DE OBJETOS DE ARTE CELEBRADA POR LA ACADEMIA DE BELLAS ARTES DE BARCELONA EN EL AÑO 1866.

CATÁLOGO DE LA EXPOSICIÓN DE OBJETOS DE ARTE, CELEBRADA EN EL EDIFICIO DE LA SOCIEDAD PARA EXPOSICIONES DE BELLAS ARTES EN BARCELONA. Barcelona, 1871.

CATÁLOGO DE LAS OBRAS DE PINTURA PERTENECIENTES AL MUSEO DE LA ACADEMIA PROVINCIAL DE BELLAS ARTES. Barcelona, 1867.

CATÁLOGO GENERAL OFICIAL DE LA EXPOSICIÓN UNIVERSAL DE BARCELONA. Barcelona, 1888.

CATÁLOGO DEL MUSEO DE BELLAS ARTES DE BARCELONA. Ayuntamiento de Barcelona, Barcelona, 1906.

CATÁLOGO GENERAL DE LA CALCOGRAFÍA NACIONAL. Real Academia de Bellas Artes de San Fernando, Madrid, 1987.

CATALUNYA EN LA ESPAÑA MODERNA. 1714-1983. Generalitat de Catalunya, Madrid, 1983.

CENTENARI DE LA SALA PARÉS. 1877-1977. Barcelona, 1977.

CIEN AÑOS DE CULTURA CATALANA. 1880-1980. Ministerio de Cultura, Madrid, 1980.

COLECCIÓN BANCO HISPANOAMERICANO. Fundación BHA, Madrid, 1991.

COLECCIÓN BANCO URQUIJO. Fundación Banco Urquijo, Madrid, 1982.

COL·LECCIONISTES D'ART A CATALUNYA. Fundació privada "Conde de Barcelona," Barcelona, 1987.

CONCURS DE PINTURA. MONTSERRAT VIST PELS PINTORS CATALANS. Barcelona, 1931-1932.

CONTEMPORARY SPANISH ART. 10 ARTISTS OF THE CATALAN SCHOOL. Ottawa, 1967-1968.

ESPAÑA A MÉXICO. MANIFESTACIÓN DE ARTE CATALÁN POR VÍCTIMAS DEL FASCISMO. AÑO 1937. 121 ARTISTAS CATALANES DE 1937. Ministerio de Cultura, Madrid, 1980.

XX.ª ESPOSIZIONE BIENNALE INTERNAZIONALE D'ARTE. CATÁLOGO DELLA MOSTRA SPAGNOLA. Venice, 1936.

EXPOSIÇÃO D'ARTE CATALÃ. Lisbon, 1921.

EXPOSICIÓ D'ART. Barcelona. (1918, 1919, 1920, 1921, 1922 and 1923).

EXPOSICIÓ D'ART CUBISTA. Galeries J. Dalmau, Barcelona, 1912.

EXPOSICIÓ DEL DIBUIX I DEL GRAVAT 1938. Barcelona, 1938.

EXPOSICIÓN BARCELONA ANTIGUA. Barcelona, 1954.

EXPOSICIÓN 100 AÑOS DE ACUARELA. AGRUPACIÓN DE ACUARELISTAS DE CATALUÑA. CENTENARIO DE LA FUNDACIÓN. Barcelona, 1965.

EXPOSICIÓN CONCURSO DE OBRAS DE ARTISTAS NOVELES. Barcelona, 1954.

EXPOSICIÓN CONCURSO NACIONAL DE ARTE EN EL DEPORTE. II JUEGOS MEDITERRÁNEOS. Barcelona, 1955.

EXPOSICIÓN DE ARTE ESPAÑOL CONTEMPORÁNEO. PINTURA Y ESCULTURA. Buenos Aires, 1947.

SEGUNDA EXPOSICIÓN DE BELLAS ARTES INAUGURADA EN DICIEMBRE DE 1884. CATÁLOGO. Galería Parés, Barcelona, 1884-1885.

III EXPOSICIÓN DE BELLAS ARTES E INDUSTRIAS ARTÍSTICAS. Barcelona, 1896.

IV EXPOSICIÓN DE BELLAS ARTES E INDUSTRIAS ARTÍSTICAS. Barcelona, 1898.

V EXPOSICIÓN DE BELLAS ARTES E INDUSTRIAS ARTÍSTICAS. Barcelona, 1907.

EXPOSICIÓN DE OBRAS PRESENTADAS AL I CONCURSO INTERNACIONAL DE DIBUJO. Fundació Ynglada-Guillot, Barcelona, 1959 et sq.

EXPOSICIÓN DE PAISAJISTAS CATALANES ORGANIZADA POR EL REAL CÍRCULO ARTÍSTICO DE BARCELONA. Madrid, 1921.

EXPOSICIÓN DE PINTURA CATALANA DESDE LA PRE-HISTORIA HASTA NUESTROS DÍAS. Ministerio de Educación Nacional, Madrid, 1962.

EXPOSICIÓN DE PINTURA CONTEMPORÁNEA. Manuel Barbié, Barcelona.

EXPOSICIÓN DE PINTURA Y ESCULTURA. Real Círculo Artístico, Barcelona, 1964.

EXPOSICIÓN DE RETRATOS Y DIBUJOS ANTIGUOS Y MODERNOS. Barcelona, 1910.

I EXPOSICIÓN GENERAL DE BELLAS ARTES. Barcelona, 1891.

II EXPOSICIÓN GENERAL DE BELLAS ARTES. Barcelona, 1897.

EXPOSICIÓN INTERNACIONAL DE ARTE. Barcelona, 1891 to 1911.

EXPOSICIÓN INTERNACIONAL DE PINTURA, ESCULTURA, DIBUJO Y GRABADO. Barcelona, 1929.

EXPOSICIÓN LEGADOS Y DONATIVOS A LOS MUSEOS DE BARCELONA. 1952-1963. Barcelona, 1963-1964.

EXPOSICIÓN MUNICIPAL DE BELLAS ARTES DE BARCELONA. Barcelona, 1951 and 1953.

EXPOSICIÓN NACIONAL DE BELLAS ARTES. Madrid, 1856 et sq.

EXPOSICIÓN NACIONAL DE BELLAS ARTES DE BARCELONA. CATÁLOGO OFICIAL. Barcelona, 1942.

EXPOSICIÓN NACIONAL DE BELLAS ARTES DE BARCELONA. CATÁLOGO OFICIAL. Barcelona, 1944.

EXPOSICIÓN REGIONAL PREPARATORIA DE LA I BIENAL HISPANOAMERICANA DE ARTE. Barcelona, 1951.

EXPOSITION INTERNATIONALE DES ARTS DÉCORATIFS ET INDUSTRIELS MODERNES. CATALOGUE DE LA SECTION ESPAGNOLE. Paris, 1925.

FONS D'ART DE LA FUNDACIÓ CAIXA DE PENSIONS. Barcelona, 1991.

GOTHSLAND. 10 ANIVERSARI. Barcelona, 1988.

GRAFISMES. 0 FIGURA, 7. Barcelona, 1963.

GRAN CERTAMEN ARTÍSTICO DE PINTURA Y ESCULTURA A BENEFICIO DEL SANTUARIO DE NUESTRA SEÑORA DEL SAGRADO CORAZÓN. Barcelona, 1944.

I GRAN EXPOSICIÓN ANUAL 1988. Sala Nonell, Barcelona, 1988.

GUASCH F., BATLLE E. *Catálogo del Museo de Arte Contemporáneo*. Barcelona, 1926.

HOMAGE TO BARCELONA. THE CITY AND ITS ART 1888-1936. Hayward Gallery, London, 1985-1986.

HOMENATGE A BARCELONA. LA CIUTAT I LES SEVES ARTS 1888-1936. Ayuntamiento de Barcelona, 1987.

HOMENATGE DE CATALUNYA A ALEXANDRE CIRICI (1914-1983). Barcelona, May-June 1984.

IDEES I ACTITUDS. EL CAMÍ DE L'ART CONCEPTUAL A CATALUNYA (1964-1980). Centre d'Art Santa Mònica, Barcelona, 1991.

INFORMALISME A CATALUNYA. PINTURA. Generalitat de Catalunya, Centre d'Art Santa Mònica, Barcelona, 1990.

ITINERARIS [I and II]. Galeria Salvador Riera, Dau al Set, Barcelona, 1991.

JOVEN FIGURACIÓN EN ESPAÑA. Barcelona, 1963.

KATALANISCHE KUNST DES 20. JAHRHUNDERTS. ART I MODERNITAT ALS PAÏSOS CATALANS. Staatliche Kunsthalle, Berlin-Barcelona, 1978.

LA CATALOGNE AUJOURD'HUI. Generalitat de Catalunya, UNESCO Palace, Paris, 1981.

LEGADO ESPONA. Barcelona, 1958.

MAN (MUESTRA DE ARTE NUEVO). Barcelona. (1962 et sq.).

MESTRES DE LA PINTURA CATALANA. Gothsland Galeria d'Art, Barcelona, Christmas 1988.

MESTRES DE LA PINTURA CATALANA. Gothsland Galeria d'Art, Barcelona, spring 1989.

EXPOSICIÓN DE ARTES SUNTUARIAS DEL MODERNISMO BARCELONÉS. J. Ainaud, J. Barbeta and M. Gil, Ayuntamiento de Barcelona, Barcelona, 1964.

EL MODERNISMO EN ESPAÑA. Madrid, 1969 - Barcelona, 1970.

EL MODERNISME. I-II. Olimpíada Cultural, Museu d'Art Modern de Barcelona, 1990-1991.

L'ÈPOCA DELS «ARTISTES». MODERNISME. NOUCENTISME. Ayuntamiento de Girona, Girona, 1991.

MOSTRA D'ART CONTEMPORANI CATALÀ. Sant Cugat del Vallès (various editions).

MUSEO ESPAÑOL DE ARTE CONTEMPORÁNEO. GUÍA CATÁLOGO. Madrid, 1975.

"NUEVAS EXPRESIONES," Sala Gaspar, Barcelona, 1966.

OBRES INCAUTADES A LA GENERALITAT DE CATALUNYA. 121 ARTISTES CATALANS. 1937. Generalitat de Catalunya y Ayuntamiento de Barcelona, Barcelona, 1980.

LA PINTURA CATALANA HOY. Museo Municipal de San Telmo, San Sebastián, 1983.

9 PINTORES CATALANES EN CUENCA. Madrid, 1978.

PINTORS I ESCULTORS CATALANS DE LA SEGONA AVANTGUARDA. Generalitat de Catalunya, Paris, 1989.

PINTURA CATALANA POSTIMPRESIONISTA. 1896-1986. Fundación Alfredo Fortabat y Amalia Lacroze de Fortabat, Buenos Aires, 1986.

PINTURA DELS DOS ÚLTIMS SEGLES. Manuel Mayoral, Barcelona, 1989.

PINTURA DELS DOS ÚLTIMS SEGLES (II). Manuel Mayoral, Barcelona, 1990.

PINTURA DELS SEGLES XIX I XX. PINTURA DE LOS SIGLOS XIX Y XX. El Corte Inglés, Barcelona, 1990.

PINTURA ESPAÑOLA DE BODEGONES Y FLOREROS. DE 1600 A GOYA. Prado, Madrid, 1983-1984.

PINTURA ORIENTALISTA ESPAÑOLA [1830/1930]. Madrid, 1988.

PREMI INTERNACIONAL DE DIBUIX JOAN MIRÓ. Barcelona, 1960 *et sq.*

PRESENCIAS DE NUESTRO TIEMPO. Galería René Metras, Barcelona (Collection).

QUATRE GATS. PRIMER SALÓN "REVISTA," Sala Parés, Barcelona, 1954.

1896-1955. RETROSPECTIVE EXHIBITION OF PAINTING FROM PREVIOUS INTERNATIONALS. Carnegie Institute, Pittsburgh, 1958-1959.

SALÓN DE OCTUBRE. [I to X. Barcelona, 1948-1957.]

RECORD DEL SALÓ D'OCTUBRE. Barcelona, 1975.

CATÀLEG DEL PRIMER SALÓ DE TARDOR ORGANITZAT PER L'ASSOCIACIÓ D'AMICS DE LES ARTS. Barcelona, December 1918.

SALÓ DE TARDOR. Barcelona, 1926.

SALÓ DE TARDOR. Barcelona, 1938.

SALÓ DE TARDOR. Ayuntamiento de Barcelona, Barcelona, 1982-1986.

I SALÓ MIRADOR. CENT ANYS DE RETRAT FEMENÍ EN LA PINTURA CATALANA 1830-1930. Barcelona, 1933.

I SALÓN DE BARCELONA DE ARTE MODERNO. Barcelona, 1960.

I SALÓ DE BARCELONA.

II SALÓ DE BARCELONA.

III SALÓ DE BARCELONA.

IV SALÓ DE BARCELONA.

V SALÓ DE BARCELONA. Barcelona, 1966.

SALÓN DE MAYO. Barcelona. (1957-1970).

SALÓ DE MONTJUÏC. Barcelona, 1936.

SALÓN FEMENINO DE ARTE ACTUAL. Barcelona (1962 *et sq.*).

I SALÓN NACIONAL DE PINTURA A LA ACUARELA. Barcelona, 1954.

UN SIGLO DE ARTE ESPAÑOL (1856-1956). Ministerio de Educación, Madrid, 1955.

UN SIGLO OLVIDADO DE PINTURA CATALANA 1750-1850. With a study by J. Subias. Amics dels Museus, Barcelona, 1951.

EL SIMBOLISMO EN LA PINTURA FRANCESA. Barcelona, 1983.

11 SPANISCHE MALER. Sala Gaspar, Frankfurt, 1959.

SURREALISME A CATALUNYA. 1924-1936. DE L'AMIC DE LES ARTS AL LOGICOFOBISME. Generalitat de Catalunya, Barcelona, May-June 1988.

TENTOONSTELLING VAN KATALAANSCHE KUNST. Holland, 1922.

20 AÑOS DE PINTURA ESPAÑOLA. Madrid, 1962.

EL VITRALL MODERNISTA. Generalitat de Catalunya, Fundació Joan Miró, Barcelona, 1984.

ELS VITRALLS CLOISONNÉ DE BARCELONA. Casa Elizalde, Ayuntamiento de Barcelona, Barcelona, 1985.

VITRALL CONTEMPORANI EN L'ARQUITECTURA. 7 ARTISTES. Ayuntamiento de Barcelona, Barcelona, June 1990.

MONOGRAPHS OF ARTISTS

EXPOSICIÓN DE ABELLÓ. Text by R. Faraldo. Galería Ramon Duran, Madrid, 1969.

EL PINTOR JOSÉ AMAT. Sala Parés, 1966.

JOSEP AMAT. EXPOSICIÓ DE PINTURES. Sala Parés, Barcelona, 1973.

FRANCESC ARTIGAU. Sala Parés, Barcelona, 1991.

BARCELÓ, BARCELONA. MIQUEL BARCELÓ PINTURES DE 1985 A 1987. Ayuntamiento de Barcelona, Barcelona, 27 November 1987 - 24 January 1988.

MIQUEL BARCELÓ IN MALI. Zurich, 1989.

EXPOSICIÓ RETROSPECTIVA DEL MALAURAT ARTISTA BARCELONÍ JOAN BRULL. Galeries Dalmau, Barcelona, 1924.

ANTONIO CABA (1838-1907) - FRANCISCO MIRALLES (1848-1901). CATÁLOGO DE LA EXPOSICIÓN. Amigos de los Museos, Galerías Layetanas, Barcelona, 1947.

EXPOSITION D'ŒUVRES DE RICARDO CANALS & NONELL-MONTURIOL. CHEZ CH. DUSBOURG. Preface by Delphi Fabrice. Galerie Le Barc de Boutteville, Paris, 1898.

CANALS. EXPOSICIÓN CONMEMORATIVA DEL CENTENARIO DE SU NACIMIENTO. Barcelona, 1976.

CASAGEMAS I EL SEU TEMPS. Daedalus, Barcelona, n.d.

EXPOSICIÓN RAMON CASAS. CATÁLOGO. Junta de Museus de Barcelona, Barcelona, 1958.

CASAS. Instituto de Cultura Hispánica, Madrid, 1965.

RAMON CASAS. Text by Joan Ainaud. Exposición Nacional de Bellas Artes, Madrid, 1968.

RAMON CASAS. 1866-1932. EXPOSICIÓN ANTOLÓGICA. Preface by Rafael Santos Torroella. Acadèmia de Belles Arts, Sabadell, 1973.

RAMON CASAS. 2 vols, Ayuntamiento de Barcelona, Barcelona, 1982-1983.

ANTONI CLAVÉ. Text by J. Cassou. Sala Gaspar, Barcelona, 1960.

CLAVÉ. 25 AÑOS DE PINTURA. Sala Gaspar, Barcelona, 7-27 May 1960.

CLAVÉ. PINTURA, COLLAGE, TAPISSERIA. Sala Gaspar, Barcelona, 1970.

ANTONI CLAVÉ. Sala Gaspar, Barcelona, 1981.

ANTONI CLAVÉ. RETORN DEL JAPÓ 1986-1987. Sala Gaspar, Barcelona, 1987.

Antoni Clavé. Exposició retrospectiva. Generalitat de Catalunya, Palau Robert, Barcelona, 18 January - 28 February 1990.

Modest Cuixart. Paintings. Bonino Gallery, New York, 1964.

Cuixart. Antològica. 1942-1975. Dau al Set, Barcelona, December 1975 - January 1976.

Modest Cuixart. Fundació Caixa de Pensions, Barcelona, 1985.

Cuixart. Pintures. 1942-1955. Dau al Set, Barcelona, 1987.

Jordi Curós. Sala Parés, Barcelona, 1991.

Exposición-homenaje al pintor J. Cusachs. Barcelona, 1965.

José Cusachs (1851-1908). Ministerio de Defensa, Madrid, 1988.

Salvador Dalí. A guide to his works in public museums. The Dalí Museum, Cleveland (Ohio), 1974.

Dalí i els llibres. Generalitat de Catalunya, Barcelona, 1982.

Salvador Dalí. 400 obres de 1914 a 1983. 2 volumes. Generalitat de Catalunya – Ministerio de Cultura, Barcelona, 1983.

Salvador Dalí. 1904-1989. Staatsgalerien, Stuttgart/Kunsthaus, Zurich, 1989.

Durancamps. Fundació Caixa de Pensions, 1990.

Feliu Elias «APA». Museu d'Art Modern, Barcelona, 1986. (Includes a complete bibliography).

Miquel Farré pintor. Generalitat de Catalunya, Barcelona, 1975.

Exposición antológica J. Fin (1916-1969). Ayuntamiento de Barcelona, Barcelona, 1971.

Fita. Pintura. 1942-1989. Diputación de Girona, 1990.

Exposición Fortuny. Ayuntamiento de Barcelona, Barcelona, 1940.

Primer centenario de la muerte de Fortuny. Text by J. Ainaud and others. Ayuntamiento de Barcelona, Barcelona, 1974.

Fortuny et ses amis français. Castres, 1974.

Fortuny 1838-1874. Fundació Caixa de Pensions, Barcelona, 1989.

Ferran Garcia Sevilla. Pintures (1987-1990). Galeria d'art Sardà i Sardà, Barcelona, May-June 1991.

Gran exposició-homenatge Francesc Gimeno (1858-1927). Olis i dibuixos. Dau al Set, Barcelona, 1978.

Donación González. Introduction, biography and catalogue by J. Ainaud, R. M. Subirana and E. Sendra. Barcelona, 1974.

Juli González. Escultures i dibuixos. Ayuntamiento de Barcelona. Barcelona, March-April 1980.

Juli González 1876-1942. Una selecció de les col·leccions de l'IVAM. Institut Valencià d'Art Modern, Caja de Ahorros de Alicante, Elche, 1988.

Xavier Gosé 1876-1915. Fundació Caixa de Pensions, Barcelona, 1984.

Guinovart: la força del llenguatge plàstic. Galeria Joan Prats, Barcelona, 1979.

Guinovart: itinerari 1948-1988. Tecla Sala, L'Hospitalet de Llobregat, November 1989-January 1990.

Manolo Hugué. Museu d'Art Modern de Barcelona, Barcelona, 1990.

Exposición Oleguer Junyent. Catálogo. Junta de Museus de Barcelona, Barcelona, 1961.

Joan Junyer. Retrospectiva. Generalitat de Catalunya, Barcelona, 1989.

Exposició homenatge a Joan Llimona en el cinquantenari de la seva mort. Sala Parés, Barcelona, 1976.

Maillol au palais des rois de Majorque. Perpignan, 1979.

Maillol 1861-1944. Fundació Caixa de Pensions, Barcelona, 1979.

Mallol Suazo. Exposició de pintures. Sala Parés, Barcelona, 1971.

Ramón Martí Alsina. Catálogo de la exposición organizada por los amigos de los museos. Biographical note by J. M. Junoy. Barcelona, 1941.

Carlos Mensa. Palma de Mallorca, 1975.

Carlos Mensa. Sala Pelaires, Palma de Mallorca, 1970.

Carlos Mensa. Ayuntamiento de Barcelona, Barcelona, May-June 1983.

Carlos Mensa. Madrid, 1987.

Centenario del nacimiento de Apeles Mestres. Ayuntamiento de Barcelona, Barcelona, 1954.

J. Mir. Exposición-homenaje. Barcelona, 1973.

Joaquim Mir (1873-1940). Exposición antológica. Dirección General de Bellas Artes, Madrid, 1971.

Joaquim Mir cinquanta anys després. Banco Bilbao Vizcaya, Barcelona, November 1990.

Joaquim Mir al camp de Tarragona. 1906-1914. Fundació "La Caixa," Barcelona, 14 May - 22 June 1991.

Soby J. T. *Joan Miró*. The Museum of Modern Art, New York, 1959.

Joan Miró: anys 20. Mutació de la realitat. Fundació Joan Miró, Barcelona, 1983.

Joan Miró. A retrospective. The Solomon R. Guggenheim Museum, New York, 1987.

Miró en las colecciones del estado. Centro de Arte Reina Sofía, Madrid, 1987.

OBRA DE JOAN MIRÓ. DIBUIXOS, PINTURA, ESCULTURA, CERÀMICA, TÈXTILS. Fundació Joan Miró, Barcelona, 1988.

IMPACTES. JOAN MIRÓ, 1929-1941. Fundació Joan Miró, 1988-1989.

ELS TALLERS DE MIRÓ. Institut Català d'Estudis Mediterranis, Barcelona, 1989.

JAUME MORERA I GALÍCIA 1854-1927. Fundació Caixa de Pensions, Barcelona, 1985.

JAUME MUXART. Sala Gaspar, Barcelona, 15-25 May 1962.

MUXART. CATÀLEG DE L'EXPOSICIÓ. Sala Gaspar, Barcelona, November-December 1988.

CARLES NADAL. Sala Parés, Barcelona, 1991.

NIEBLA. PINTURA ENCARA. Tecla Sala, L'Hospitalet de Llobregat, September-October 1990.

EXPOSICIÓN XAVIER NOGUÉS. BARCELONA 1873-1941. CATÁLOGO. Ayuntamiento de Barcelona, Barcelona, March-April 1967.

LEGADO ISABEL ESCALADA VDA. XAVIER NOGUÉS. Barcelona, 1972.

EXPOSICIÓN ISIDRE NONELL. CATÁLOGO. Junta de Museus de Barcelona, Barcelona, 1961.

ISIDRE NONELL. Exposición Nacional de Bellas Artes, Madrid, 1966.

NONELL. Ayuntamiento de Barcelona, 16 June-31 August 1981.

NONELL. Madrid, 1981.

JOSEP OBIOLS. Ayuntamiento de Barcelona, Barcelona, 1990.

EXPOSICIÓN HOMENAJE A SANT-YAGO PADRÓS ELÍAS. Terrassa, 1973.

JORDI PERICOT. Barcelona, 1972.

PICASSO. ŒUVRES REÇUES EN PAIEMENT DES DROITS DE SUCCESSION. Ministère de la Culture et de la Communication, Grand Palais, Paris, 11 October 1979-7 January 1980.

PABLO PICASSO. A RETROSPECTIVE. Museum of Modern Art, New York, 1980.

PICASSO I BARCELONA. 1881-1981. Barcelona, 1981-1982.

PICASSO 1881-1973. EXPOSICIÓN ANTOLÓGICA. Madrid, 1981 – Museu Picasso de Barcelona, 1982.

MUSEU PICASSO. CATÀLEG DE PINTURA I DIBUIX. Ayuntamiento de Barcelona, Barcelona, 1984.

JE SUIS LE CAHIER. THE SKETCHBOOKS OF PICASSO. Royal Academy of Arts, London, 1986.

MUSÉE PICASSO. PARÍS. CATÁLOGO DE LAS COLECCIONES. Introduction by Dominique Bozo. Catalogue by Marie-Laure Besnard-Bernadac, Michelle Richet, Hélène Seckel. Biography by Laurence Marceillac. Ed. Polígrafa, Barcelona, 1985.

EXPOSICIÓN PIDELASERRA. CATÁLOGO. Museu d'Art Modern de Barcelona, Barcelona, 1948.

MARIÀ PIDELASERRA. IMPRESSIONISME I PUNTILLISME. Galeria Arturo Ramon, Barcelona, 1975.

JOAN PONÇ 1946-1970. Galeria René Metras (Presencias de nuestro tiempo), Barcelona, 1972.

JOAN PONÇ. Dau al Set, Barcelona, 1976.

JOAN PONÇ. FONS DE L'ÉSSER. Galeria Joan Prats, Barcelona, 1978. (With an autobiographical chronology).

JOAN PONÇ. DIBUIXOS 1946-1949. Dau al Set, Barcelona, 1987.

EXPOSICIÓ PONS MARTÍ. 1855-1931. Girona, 1973.

RÀFOLS CASAMADA. EXPOSICIÓ ANTOLÒGICA. 1957-1985. Generalitat de Catalunya, Fundació Joan Miró, Barcelona, 1985-1986.

MARIA ASSUMPCIÓ RAVENTÓS. OBRES 1950-1987. Ayuntamiento de Sant Sadurní d'Anoia, 1987.

EXPOSICIÓN RENART. Ayuntamiento de Barcelona, Museus d'Art, Barcelona, 1965-1966.

ALEXANDRE DE RIQUER. 1856-1920. Caixa de Barcelona. Barcelona, 1985.

EXPOSICIÓ DEL CINQUANTENARI DE LA MORT DE SANTIAGO RUSIÑOL. Text ("Assaig sobre les diferents etapes pictòriques") by Isabel Coll. Palau Maricel, Sitges, 1981.

SANTIAGO RUSIÑOL. EXPOSICIÓ ANTOLÒGICA. Barcelona, 1981.

CENTENARI SAMARRA 1886-1986. Lleida-Ponts, 1986.

JOSÉ MARIA SERT 1874-1945. Ministerio de Cultura, Madrid, 1987. Barcelona, 1988.

DE SUCRE. Text by D. Giralt-Miracle. Dau al Set, Barcelona, 1990.

JOAQUIM SUNYER 1874-1956. Fundació Caixa de Pensions, Barcelona, 1983.

J. M. TAMBURINI. Text by J. Soler. Fundació Caixa de Barcelona, Barcelona, 1989.

TÀPIES. ELS ANYS 80. Ayuntamiento de Barcelona, Barcelona, 1988.

TÀPIES I BARCELÓ. Text by V. Combalia. Galeria d'Art Sardà i Sardà, Barcelona, 1990.

TÀPIES. EXTENSIONS DE LA REALITAT. Fundació Joan Miró, Barcelona, 28 February-14 April 1991.

EXPOSICIÓ ANTOLÒGICA DE L'OBRA DE J. J. THARRATS. Fontana d'Or. Girona, spring 1975.

J. J. THARRATS. MACULATURES. 1950-1965. Figueres, 1990.

THARRATS. OBRA GRÀFICA 1957-1990. Barcelona, 1990.

FRANCESC TODÓ. 30 PINTURES. 1946-1984. Tortosa, 1984.

FRANCESC TODÓ. Sala Parés, Barcelona, 1990.

PERE TORNÉ ESQUIUS. Text by F. Miralles. Barcelona, 1987.

Francisco Torras y Armengol (1832-1878). Ayuntamiento de Terrassa, Terrassa, 1916.

J. Torres-Garcia (1874-1940). Exposición antológica. Museo Español de Arte Contemporáneo, Madrid, April-May 1973.

Torres-Garcia. Escultura-dibuix-símbol. Fundació Joan Miró, Barcelona, 13 March-4 May 1986.

Joaquín Torres-Garcia. Marianovich Arte, Barcelona, 1990.

Xavier Valls. Museu d'Art Modern, Barcelona, 1985.

Vallsquer. Casa Elizalde, Barcelona, 1987.

Vayreda Canadell. Sala Nonell, Barcelona, 1975.

Vayreda's. Palau de Caramany, Girona, 1975.

Exposició A. Vila Arrufat. Acadèmia de Belles Arts de Sabadell, Sabadell, 1973.

Viladecans. Peintures sur papier 1980-1981. Centre d'Etudes Catalanes, Paris, 1982.

Viladecans. Sala Gaspar, Barcelona, 1987.

Vila-Puig. 1890-1990. Manel Mayoral, Barcelona, 1990.

Miquel Villà. Antològica. 1926-1977. Dau al Set, Barcelona, 1977.

Miquel Villà. Exposició antològica. Obra de 1917 a 1985. Generalitat de Catalunya, Barcelona, 1985.

Els llibres de Zush. Generalitat de Catalunya, Centre d'Art Santa Mònica, Barcelona, June-July 1989.

LIST OF ILLUSTRATIONS

Note: all dimensions are given in centimetres, height followed by width.
Photo credits for all photographs from the Museum of Modern Art, Barcelona: Photo Antón Oromí.